The Rise and Fall
of Mass Communication

Mass
Communication
and
Journalism

Lee B. Becker
General Editor

Vol. 27

The Mass Communication and Journalism series
is part of the Peter Lang Media and Communication list.
Every volume is peer reviewed and meets the highest
quality standards for content and production.

PETER LANG
New York • Bern • Berlin
Brussels • Vienna • Oxford • Warsaw

William L. Benoit and Andrew C. Billings

The Rise and Fall
of Mass Communication

PETER LANG

New York • Bern • Berlin
Brussels • Vienna • Oxford • Warsaw

Library of Congress Cataloging-in-Publication Data
Names: Benoit, William L., author. | Billings, Andrew C., author.
Title: The rise and fall of mass communication /
William L. Benoit and Andrew C. Billings.
Description: New York: Peter Lang, 2020.
Series: Mass communication and journalism; vol. 27 | ISSN 2153-2761
Includes bibliographical references and index.
Identifiers: LCCN 2020006005 (print) | LCCN 2020006006 (ebook)
ISBN 978-1-4331-6426-2 (hardback: alk. paper)
ISBN 978-1-4331-6422-4 (paperback: alk. paper) | ISBN 978-1-4331-6423-1 (ebook pdf)
ISBN 978-1-4331-6424-8 (epub) | ISBN 978-1-4331-6425-5 (mobi)
Subjects: LCSH: Mass media—Audiences. | Consumers' preferences—United
States. | Mass media—United States—History.
Classification: LCC P96.A83 B46 2020 (print) | LCC P96.A83 (ebook)
DDC 302.23—dc23
LC record available at https://lccn.loc.gov/2020006005
LC ebook record available at https://lccn.loc.gov/2020006006
DOI 10.3726/b16805

Bibliographic information published by **Die Deutsche Nationalbibliothek.**
Die Deutsche Nationalbibliothek lists this publication in the "Deutsche
Nationalbibliografie"; detailed bibliographic data are available
on the Internet at http://dnb.d-nb.de/.

The paper in this book meets the guidelines for permanence and durability
of the Committee on Production Guidelines for Book Longevity
of the Council of Library Resources.

© 2020 Peter Lang Publishing, Inc., New York
29 Broadway, 18th floor, New York, NY 10006
www.peterlang.com

Printed in the United States of America

Table of Contents

List of Tables

List of Figures

Preface

Inspiration struck at a Red Lobster. As Bill had recently moved nearby to Andy, we met for lunch to catch up. When turning thoughts to research, Bill mentioned that he felt one article he was inspired to write pertained to the decline of what we always thought of as mass communication. It was not the death of media, we both agreed, but it was a new era in which one had to reconsider what a "mass" audience was. Andy replied that he was studying similar principles in entertainment media, noting the relative lack of watercooler programs except for a *Bachelor* episode or key awards show. We discovered that we were both intrigued by the same principles: niches, customization, narrowcasting and what we eventually advance here: media balkanization theory. We also realized that if we connected all of these principles of news and entertainment, we did not merely have a journal article on our hands but, rather, a book project. That vision became *The Rise and Fall of Mass Communication*.

Bill would like to thank his wife, Pam Benoit, and their daughter, Jen Benoit-Bryan, for their support and inspiration. He would also like to thank Andy for his help and work on our book. Andy wishes to thank his wife, Angela, and his two sons, Nathan and Noah, who frequently were the sounding board for new book ideas and examples. He also wishes to thank Bill for being a terrific writing partner.

The Rise and Fall of Mass Communication traverses considerable ground, chronicling the rise of different media products—each with their pinnacles at slightly different times, news in the 1960s, music albums in the late 1970s, scripted television in the 1980s. However, each balkanized in the era of the Internet, with that splintering still occurring today. That apex and decline, we feel, is worthy of documentation. By the time you finish this book, we hope you agree.

Introduction: The Rise and Fall of Mass Communication

On February 28, 1983, Americans tuned in to what was later dubbed "a watershed moment in the history of American pop culture" (Freeman, 2018, para. 1). The CBS series *M*A*S*H* was completing its 11-year run and people flocked to witness the fates of Hawkeye, Houlihan, Klinger, and the rest of the 4077th Mobile Army Surgical Hospital. The audience was epic (106 million viewers), swelling to 121.6 million if including all who watched at least six minutes of the finale (Campbell, 2019). America (population 233 million) experienced a shared cultural moment, discussing it the next day and referencing it for years to come.

Thirty-six years later, America (now with an extra 98 million in population) tuned in again for what was, without question, the most viewed and beloved comedy program of the decade. Chuck Lorre's CBS series *The Big Bang Theory* was completing a block buster run in 2019, being the highest-rated-situation comedy for seven of its 12 years of existence, including the 2018–2019 broadcast season. The finale, hailed by most critics as both satisfying and fun, was a capper that most fans could support. Deadline's Geoff Boucher (2019) dubbed it a "picture perfect landing" with "satisfying surprises for all of the core characters" (para. 1). There was just one demerit to place on the series finale: it was not, even remotely, watched by a mass audience commensurate with *M*A*S*H* or other beloved sitcoms of the past, with just 18 million viewers tuning in to find out how Sheldon, Leonard, and the gang's storylines would conclude (Fitzgerald, 2019). Instead of garnering half

Table 1. Television Finale Viewership by Population Percentage (Watson, 2019)

Program	Year	Viewers (millions)	% of U.S. Population
M*A*S*H	1983	106	45.5
Cheers	1994	80.4	30.9
Seinfeld	1998	76	27.5
Friends	2004	52.5	17.9
The Big Bang Theory	2019	18	5.4

the population, *Big Bang* had secured just 5.4% of all Americans for its finale and yet, in CBS' estimation of the media landscape, it was still a ratings success.

Placing the ratings of *The Big Bang Theory* alongside other finales, the comparisons are startling:

As Figure 1 then shows, these figures become even more stark when considering the growth in the overall population (from 233 million in 1983 to 331 million in 2019).

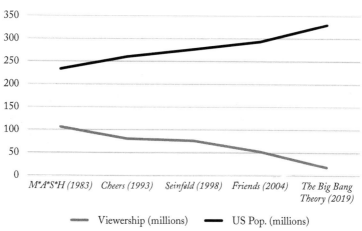

Figure 1. Seminal Television Finales (1983–2019)

Where had the audience gone? Other 2019 television touchstones faced similar ratings challenges based on their own previous benchmarks. The Super Bowl drew 100.7 million viewers, yet would be the lowest Super Bowl rating in over a decade. The State of the Union, delayed one week due to a government shutdown, would attract 46.8 million viewers (Porter, 2019a), a far cry from the record of 66.9 million viewers set by President Bill Clinton in 1993. Then came the Oscars, replete with more popular Best Picture nominees than most years (including *Black Panther* and *Bohemian Rhapsody*), scoring its second-lowest audience ever with 29.6 million viewers (Otterson, 2019). And yet, people were not abandoning television; the average American watched over six hours per day, aligned with the highest of any year. The audience was splintering, though, with only the Super Bowl able to garner more than 15% of the 331 million people residing in the United States. When *M*A*S*H* had its finale, 45% of all Americans tuned in whereas when *The Big Bang Theory* had its finale, just 5% of all Americans watched. The contrast is as stark as it is dramatic.

For instance, Stelter (2015) observed that FOX's 2016 GOP debate "was watched by 24 million viewers on Thursday night, according to Nielsen data, making it the highest-rated primary debate in television history." This audience was unusually large: The audience easily exceeded pretty much everything that's been on American television this year, from the finale of *The Walking Dead* to the final episode of David Letterman's *Late Show*. The debate was bigger than all of this year's NBA Finals and MLB World Series games, and most of the year's NFL match-ups. It also trumped Jon Stewart's Thursday night's sign-off from *The Daily Show*, which averaged 3.5 million viewers.

Although this is debate attained an historic high for primary debate viewers, keep in mind that in 2015 the U.S. population was 321 million and 87 million people identified as Republicans (Gallup, 2019). Many people watched this debate (and others), but it still did not reach most voters—or even most Republican voters.

One could assume this is the result of cord-cutting, combined with online media content distribution and both, to some degree, play a role. However, while eyeballs went elsewhere, mass eyeballs watching the same content in the same way at the same time as in the heydays of mass communication in the 1970s cannot be found anywhere on the modern media palate. We were witnessing the "end of shared civic reality" (Tolentino, 2019, p. 30). The great splintering of mass communication had begun.

Devices, Platforms, and Networks

This is not a story merely of television. Nor is it a tale solely of legacy media being replaced by online options. Yes, media such as radio and newspapers have been inordinately diminished, yet understandings of what replaced it are far less linear than previous platitudes suggested in a song such as *Video Killed the Radio Star*. Figure 2 tells the stories of newspapers, which grew to steady circulations of households throughout the 1970s and 80s, and then declined to half that number in recent years ("Newspapers Fact Sheet," 2019)—with more drops seemingly inevitable.

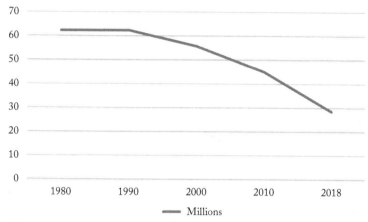

Figure 2. Newspaper Circulation by Year (Weekday)

A similar story can be found with the evening news. As Figure 3 shows, at its peak in 1980, the three broadcast networks' nightly news broadcasts accounted for 75% of all timeslot viewership ("The Transformation of Network News," 1999); that number is now one quarter of that share (Statista, 2016).

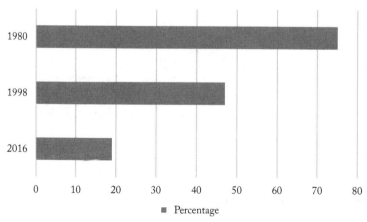

Figure 3. Percentage Televisions Tuned Evening Broadcast Nightly News

Those who might think that cable news is the culprit can think again; even when including FOX News, CNN, and MSNBC, that collective proportion (broadcast and cable combined) rises only to 9.5%. A 1973 Oliver Quayle poll found 90% of Americans could recognize CBS News anchor Walter Cronkite (Bowman, 2009); imagine what the percentage would be for today's hosts, Lester Holt, David Muir, and Norah O'Donnell.

Yet what is more intriguing for the purposes of this book is that each of these highly-consumed platforms was essentially replaced by dozens of others, each serving a smaller fraction of the audience Walter Cronkite used to enjoy on CBS. In the process: "did you see that?" was largely replaced in the cultural lexicon with "don't tell me, I may watch it later," as one largely presumes that an individual's media diet is as unique as it is massive.

In this process, notions of things such as channels and networks (NBC, CBS, ABC) have become virtually indecipherable from platforms (live, streaming, mobile) and devices (television, tablets, laptops, phones). The permutations of use become so indecipherable that one often renders media content in a binary manner: yes, I know what program you're talking about or no, I'm not familiar with that program. One of the primary tenets of this book is that such distinctions matter. The contrast between when a person reads a tweet along with its full thread is significant than when another person sees that same tweet repeated on someone else's social media feed. The difference between watching *Breaking Bad* in steady, live television-based installments over the course of five years is noteworthy when compared to someone who binges the entire series over their phone on a cross-country bus trip. The between reading a book in hard copy in its first week of release is a different experience than when one reads it on their tablet many years later.

Many books are now written about the new opportunities forged by a niche media economy; this book is one of the few to focus on what was lost in the process. It is not a lament—as options are good—but it is a sense of loss about some common language, common conversation, and common sets of facts and realities. As *Entertainment Weekly* (now offered monthly due to its own changing industry models) editor J. D. Heyman (2019) contends:

> I wouldn't trade this era for any other. But every so often, I do yearn for the days when TV was our sketchy little hearth, connecting us to a few things, all at the exact same time. (Missed it? Wait for summer reruns.) There's a story Tina Fey tells that makes my heart clench, about being a kid on Saturday nights, sipping cream soda out of a champagne glass and wearing her mom's caftan so she could pretend she was on the lido deck when *The Love Boat* aired. Yeah, it was dumb, but it was magic: all of us lonely kids, glued to the box. It held us close, linked us together, and in its lovable, tacky way, made us a bit more whole. (p. 7)

Heyman's thoughts (and seemingly some of Fey's as well) largely mirror our inspirations for this book, not just about television, but about virtually every media option in the modern landscape. The book focuses on what is gained and lost when one customizes their media world and, in doing so, ends the era of mass media—at least when using the typical definition of a message communicated to a large group of people in the same way at the same time. It is, we contend, a worthwhile endeavor to examine the benefits and drawbacks of replacing key, shared moments with individual, isolated, targeted content seemingly made exactly for you, the individual, more than any large swath of the population.

The Role of Cultural Touchstones

With arguably one of the most inventive cinematic hooks of the year 2019, screenwriter Richard Curtis penned a movie, *Yesterday*, that offered an intriguing premise: what if the world suddenly changed and no one but you had ever heard of the Beatles (and their legendary catalogue of hits)? Other aspects of culture were removed in the film and some could be argued for the better: *Yesterday* featured a world without cigarettes, responsible for 480,000 deaths in the United States alone ("Fast Facts," 2018). However, the reality imagined in the film lacked both the Beatles and *Harry Potter* novels, and a world without "I Want to Hold Your Hand" or the magic of Dumbledore seemed a cold one. As main character Jack Malik reintroduces Beatles music to the world, cultural touchstones are embedded; the ability to sing or hum a song collectively created a pseudo-shared language for people around the globe.

This film underscores the value of commonality. We may be fragmented into millions of conversations and interests, yet if seeking for a topic of conversation at a party or business dinner, one could rely on these touchstones as fallback plans—heuristics in which societal experience is somewhat shared. Whether these touchstones should be valued over individually-appealing content is of considerable debate among media critics. One, *TIME* magazine's Judy Berman (2019), believes an "entertainment monoculture" (p. 52) is undesirable because, she contends, although it is:

… nice to have a show that can serve as the cultural lingua franca, especially now that Americans of different ages, races, religions, countries of origin, genders, sexualities and education levels seem to so often misunderstand each other, [but] if consensus is the price of variety and visibility, I'm happy to pay it. (p. 53)

Others are less sanguine. *Wired*'s Emily Dreyfuss (2019) used the series finale of HBO's *Game of Thrones* to lament the end of "the world of communal television" (para. 12). The quandary within this new media landscape is that while audiences are splintering, they still—just as much as ever before—seek to know what others are consuming. The need to know the popular (and the pop culture reference or meme accompanying it) are still essential to modern communication. The modicum from *Wired* magazine editor Chris Anderson (2006) still holds today: "The tracking of top seller hits is a national obsession. Our culture is a massive popularity contest. We are consumed by hits—making them, choosing them, talking about them, and following their rise and fall … Hits, in short, *rule*" (p. 1).

What happens when hits are not really "hits" in the traditional sense? We merely act like they are. Importance is attached to content that may not be as singularly powerful as one thinks. Liberals lament the outsized influence of people like FOX News host Sean Hannity on his self-monikered program, *Hannity* (garnering 0.9% of the American public at 9 p.m. ET each night; Joyella, 2019) while conservatives believe outlets such as *The Daily Show with Trevor Noah* (with 0.2% of Americans watching him live each night; Welch, 2019) give liberals their marching orders. Certainly, these audiences matter as they represent more people than would have been necessary to tip the results of the 2016 Presidential election, yet a sense of widespread perspective is nonetheless lost. One assumes there is something everyone is watching or reading when, almost every week, nothing matches this description. Please note that we are not arguing the end of media, or media influence. However, the concept of "mass media" somehow seemed redundant before, as all media was intended (and received because of limited outlets) for mass audiences. However, can we truly call something "mass" when the supposed influence leader, FOX News, is reaching an average of less than 1% of the population at any one time?

Social media "trending" is constantly making mountains out of molehills. Why? Because news media has been built on one premise: you report on mountains. There *must* be mountains.

And there are … a few. Even then, there are some asterisks.

The Hits that Remain: Power, Yet Nuanced Impact

Of course, one could maintain we have selective amnesia and that massive media events occur even if not the projectable television-based ones. One could ask: if all audience is fragmented, how does *Game of Thrones* garner the most single-week viewership of any episode in the history of HBO (Porter, 2019b)? Yet we could counter that while many watched *GoT*, they did so on their own time in a variety of formats (live, DVR, a dozen repeat airings on a multitude of HBO channels, HBO Go [for cable/satellite subscribers on the go], HBO Now [for non-cable/satellite subscribers still on the go]), as well as bootlegged copies and shared password views). So, yes, people watched *GoT*, but with dramatically different formats, times, and devices—and even then, HBO only boasts 42 million subscribers, meaning this was a phenomenon to which the majority did not even have access.

But was not the highest grossing film of all-time, *Avengers: Endgame*, during this same time period? Yes, it was. However, its domestic gross ($858M) is measured in dollars, not number of tickets sold. Once adjusted for inflation, the film drops to outside of the top ten all-time—not bad, but also not revolutionary. *Gone with the Wind* still topples the Avengers once one makes such an adjustment and nary a film from the 21st Century makes the top-ten list. In the 1930s, 65% of Americans attended films weekly (Koszarski, 1990); meanwhile, an estimated 12% of Americans watched *Avengers: Endgame* on opening weekend. Among that 12% of the American population, the experiences ranged quite noticeably, including 3D, IMAX, D-Box, 3D IMAX, and other theatre conveniences that were present for some and yet not for others. The person witnessing the film in 3D IMAX with concierge service and deluxe sound on an opening Thursday night probably had a demonstrably different experience than the person at the 11 a.m. Sunday show at a 2D rural theatre with no major updates in many decades.

The fact that sports audiences for many of the major American sporting events (NBA Finals, The Masters, Kentucky Derby) are largely the same now as a decade ago shows their amplified importance. With everything else shrinking, it is fair to observe that sports are the primary source of the live mass media events. As the saying goes, in the land of the blind, the one-eyed man is king. In this new media landscape, sports are, indeed, the king atop the pinnacle of the melting mountain.

Consequently, there are multiple permutations of the rise and fall of mass communication, including whether someone witnessed the same media product as someone else as the manner in which that media product was consumed even if viewed en masse.

The Age of Infinite Media Choice: Fragmentation of Audience Selections and Tastes

Fragmentation of media options was not the first element of society to begin to splinter toward specific tastes and away from mass produced centrist products; many other industries experienced this decades ago. In 1974, the fast food burger chain Burger King released a highly successful advertising campaign: "Have it Your Way" (McCarthy, 2005). The concept was simple: mass produced burgers with a set combination of condiments were out; in was a new mechanism for creating one's own optimal burger experience. With a catchy tagline "Your way, right away at Burger King now," the campaign was successful—and the "right away" portion of the line was designed to indicate speed of receiving one's food would not be impeded. Other fast food restaurants followed suit, expanding menus and specializing in customization in ways the industry had never before witnessed.

The result was a populace that continually found new demands for specialization, Starbucks orders that take up to 20 seconds just to recite, and the eventual slowing down of the core assembly line mechanism.

Other industries were following suit: sports stadiums that used to either be general seating or similar seating (albeit from differing qualities of vantage points) were adding luxury boxes in the 1970s and, by the 1990s, club suites and other experiences. Airlines with standard amenities within flights began adding amenities for first class passengers while simultaneously subtracting them for others. The results were similar in most of these cases: a plethora of options begat dissimilar experiences, whether separated by taste, priorities, or economic means. Common touchpoints were replaced with widening cultural experiences. An "us" who had experienced something similar; a much larger group of "them" that had not.

What is lost seems minor: the commonality of what it means to eat a burger, attend a game, or fly on an airplane. Yet, these experiences form a society's language; that joke about "airline food" might now fall flat as the concept now widely varies. Media used to be segmented by demographics. "Soul charts" racially divided music tastes and film ratings somewhat segmented the ages. However, when the ability to sort oneself is combined with ubiquity of media options, demographics are superseded by tastes that may or may not match the demographic in which one was previously classified. Marketing expert Chris Riley claimed that Nike and Apple stopped asking for demographic-based marketing because "they don't trust it … there is no [demographic] category for somebody who shapes his entire life around his concern for the environment." Hence, the big sort begat the big customization.

Two books of the aughts captured the zeitgeist that fostered the fall of mass communication. One was Chris Anderson's *The Long Tail: Why the Future of Business is Selling Less of More* (2006). Anderson advanced the case that a "mass of niches has always existed, but as the cost of reaching it falls—consumers finding niche products, and niche products finding consumers—it's suddenly becoming a cultural and economic force to be reckoned with" (p. 6). Put simply, the focus had previously been on the middle of the bell curve, the mass where all of the hits reside and watercooler conversation took place. Now, with a world of ubiquitous access to content, the tails of the curve move to the fore; the curve flattens and the "mass" in the center is no longer as valued. Anderson (2006) explains the new niche market:

> Think of these falling distribution costs as a dropping waterline or a receding tide. As they fall, they reveal a new land that has been there all along, just underwater … They are the movies that didn't make it to your local theater, the music not played on the local rock radio station, the sports equipment not sold at Wal-Mart. (p. 6)

In sum, Anderson argues that the massive, uber-popular media offering used to rule the roost, yet now occupied a much more crowded space where niches could eventually subsume, blunt, or overwhelm the mass.

The other telling book was Bill Bishop's (2009) entry, *The Big Sort: Why the Clustering of Like-Minded America is Tearing Us Apart*. Documenting a series of processes from the early 1970s to 2004, Bishop contended that people were (typically unconsciously) sorting themselves into homogenous communities. Yes, these were political divides Bishop was delineating, but they became lifestyle divides. Jenson (2013) found in a Public Policy Polling report that this even affected eating habits. Republicans eat Papa John's Pizza; Democrats prefer Pizza Hut. Democrats got their chicken at KFC; Republicans strongly preferred Chick-Fil-A. These then percolate within geographic imprints; liberal New York City, for instance, got its first Chick-Fil-A in 2015 (Stafford, 2015), 69 years and over 2,000 franchises after the company was established. Yes, in an era where interests can be matched with geography, the nation's most populous city had to wait while places like Brandon, Mississippi and Sumter, South Carolina were served first. In essence, Bishop was reporting on how demographic shifts changed entire environments, customizing them for the precise sliver of America calling it home.

Notice that both books lead with the post-colon of *why* something is happening. They are not arguing that it was avoidable, or even should be avoided or amended. Rather, both Anderson and Bishop make the case for the inevitable: Delivery of media content reached zero while mobility and a variety of other technological affordances allowed people to cluster with people in which they were most comfortable. Galloway (2018) even argues that in some industries, "the long tail is growing. Thus, it's better to work at Google than a niche search player, but conversely, it's better to work for a craft brewery than for Miller ... the long tail has new life in consumers, as discretionary income wants special, not big" (pp. 243–244). *The Long Tail* was about the ability to sort media for optimal consumption; *The Big Sort* was about the desire to do so. As Bishop (2009) writes, "freed from want and worry, people were reordering their lives around their values, their tastes, and their beliefs" (p. 12). Both trends were inevitable. So, too, was the eventual fall of mass communication.

Ultimately, this book is used to agree with both Bishop (that sorting was inevitable) and Anderson (that all the niches representing the long tail can add up to more than the core/center). However, the mere ability to amalgamate a media audience of eyeballs should not be equated to substituting for the mass collective audience it replaces. People can consume just as much (if not more) media than before but, because of fragmentation, the loss is common experience and other interactive elements. And those commonalities become more problematic when common facts and statistics are no longer shared. Decades after the late Senator Patrick Moynihan was attributed to saying that one is "everyone is entitled to their own opinions, but they are not entitled to their own facts," it appears that many now disagree—creating and staying within one's own echo chamber.

The Rise of Ideologically Conflicting News

Mass communication is best conceptualized as a message that reaches (is consumed by) a large number of people (we do not propose a precise cutoff point). The rise of mass communication is enabled by two factors: population growth (more potential audience members) and advances in communication technology (moving from face-to-face to writing to the printing press to radio to television to the Internet and social media). Thus, we argue (along with Prior, 2007) that the apex of mass communication—particularly when measured by the percentage of the potential audience that consume a message—came in the 1960s and 1970s, with the heyday of broadcast television. However, as more choices arose (new networks via satellite or cable TV, new media from technological advances), the audience reached by any given message shrank. The recent increasing ideological divide exacerbates this trend as people seek out media with a particular slant. This means that we have moved from people who have a relatively similar world view to a multitude of groups consuming different and conflicting messages.

Increasingly, we find individuals claiming to be well-informed, yet with ever-expanding lists of sources that are used to accomplish this aim. These sources are increasingly customized to fit pre-existing world views, creating the "thought bubbles" that are pervasive talking points in our current news era. If one does not enjoy a given news source, it is often discarded in favor of a more pleasurable one. Yet Barnidge et al. (2020) ask the pertinent question: "If the individuals who are most likely to perceive media bias no longer encounter, via selective exposure, media content they might consider biased, why are perceptions of media bias so pervasive?" The answer, they argue, lies in the positive relationship between political extremity and selective exposure. The more media there is in which to choose, the more selective exposure there can be.

This unfurls online in peculiar ways in regard to knowledge. Panek, Hollenbach, Yang, and Rhodes (2018) utilize a study of Reddit to show that as groups grow in size, participation becomes more concentrated among select individuals. As much as we might wish to call the Internet the great democratizer where everyone has an equal voice, groups still function as they always have, focusing a conversation and priorities where opinion leaders desire. This book will certainly explore these elements as they relate to news and general forms of modern information literacy, imperatives in the world, we argue, as media fragmentation scatters not only our interests, but also our priorities.

Book Overview

Thus, we have prepared a book that unfolds first with a sense of history, then with two primary prongs of fragmentation, then with principles that apply within both prongs, and finally with a theory for understanding our splintering world.

Chapter 1 chronicles the rise of mass communication, showing how concentrated audiences were for evening news and print sources as well as for entertainment offerings that achieved astounding audience penetration.

The next two chapters then document the fall of mass communicated news (Chapter 2) and entertainment (Chapter 3). Each have distinct paths of dispersion, yet key moments for both will be argued to be the rise of cable TV, the Internet, and mobile media devices.

Chapter 4 then explores the role of customization in media, as content producers wisely discovered that the ability to offer hundreds (and then thousands, and then millions) of content channels should not result in delivering the same content over and over to the masses, but to differentiate that content for smaller groups that will become both more engaged and more loyal. Chapter 5 then begins to turn to what is lost in this customization process, namely that society insists on cultural barometers that apply to mass groups (if not the whole country), even if such applications are a fool's errand when any form of media content (sans a Super Bowl or Presidential Debate), draws what could be constituted as a mass audience anymore. The loss of the watercooler effect is then advanced in Chapter 6, noting that while most report a high level of enjoyment with the myriad options micro-targeted to their desires, rarely can those form cultural touchstones of widespread conversation.

All of these pieces build to our ultimate chapter, Chapter 7, which advances our new theory, media balkanization, based on six axioms for not only navigating a balkanized media environment, but for reconsidering the majority of our core communication theories in the process—particularly the effects-based theories, often founded on the notion of a mass audience, which we contend now rarely is attained.

In the end, we must stress the notion once more that we are not arguing that the current media environment is better or worse than the stages preceding it. You will find ample evidence for both the strengths and weaknesses of where we find ourselves today. Walter Miller, in his 1959 classic book, *A Canticle for Leibowitz*, writes that "he did not like saying it. To communicate a fact seemed always to lend it fuller existence." When we speak of the "rise and fall of mass communication" with our friends and colleagues, they typically sound intrigued, but first sigh at the prospect, as the first response tends to be to lament the lost past. However, we simply wish to acknowledge the fuller existence of balkanized media, a conception that has rocked the foundation of mass communication.

References

Anderson, C. (2006). *The long tail: Why the future of business is selling less of more.* New York: Hatchette.

Barnidge, M., Gunther, A. C., Kim, J., Hong, Y., Perryman, M., Tay, S. K., & Knisely, S. (2020). Politically motivated selective exposure and perceived media bias. *Communication Research.* Available via online first, last accessed on March 24, 2020: https://journals.sagepub.com/doi/abs/10.1177/0093650217713066.

Berman, J. (2019, May 27). 'Game of Thrones' is over. Is that so bad? *Time, 97,* p. 52–53.

Bishop, B. (2009). *The big sort: Why the clustering of like-minded America is tearing us apart.* Boston: Houghton Mifflin.

Boucher, G. (2019, May 16). 'Big Bang Theory' ends 12-year run with eye on the prize (& big surprise guest. *Deadline.* Retrieved on March 24, 2020 at: https://deadline.com/2019/05/big-bang-theory-ends-12-year-run-with-eye-on-the-prize-big-surprise-guest-1202616618/.

Bowman, K. (2009, July 27). The decline of the major networks. *Forbes.* Retrieved on March 24, 2020 at: https://www.forbes.com/2009/07/25/media-network-news-audience-opinions-columnists-walter-cronkite.html#31e687b147a5.

Campbell, C. (2019, May 21). 'Goodbye, Farewell and Amen' remains the king of TV series finales. *Film School Rejects.* Retrieved on March 24, 2020 at: https://filmschoolrejects.com/goodbye-farewell-and-amen-remains-the-king-of-tv-series-finales/.

Dreyfuss, E. (2019, May 16). 'Game of Thrones' is the last great show to bring us together. *Wired.* Retrieved on March 24, 2020 at: https://www.wired.com/story/game-of-thrones-watercooler-show/.

"Fast Facts" (2018, November 28). Smoking and tobacco use. *Centers for Disease Control and Prevention.* Retrieved on March 24, 2020 at: https://www.cdc.gov/tobacco/data_statistics/fact_sheets/fast_facts/index.htm.

Fitzgerald, T. (2019, May 17). How do 'The Big Bang Theory' series finale ratings rank all time? *Forbes.* Retrieved on March 24, 2020 at: https://www.forbes.com/sites/tonifitzgerald/2019/05/17/how-does-the-big-bang-theory-series-finale-ratings-rank-all-time/#2667639f386d.

Freeman, M. (2018, February 22). M*A*S*H finale, 35 years later: Untold stories of one of TV's most important shows. *The Hollywood Reporter.* Retrieved on March 24, 2020 at: https://www.hollywoodreporter.com/features/mash-oral-history-untold-stories-one-tvs-important-shows-1086322.

Galloway, S. (2018). *The four: The hidden DNA of Amazon, Apple, Facebook, and Google.* New York: Penguin.

Gallup (2019). Party affiliation. *Gallup.* Retrieved on March 24, 2020 at: https://news.gallup.com/poll/15370/partyaffiliation.aspx.

Heyman, J. D. (2019, October). A new golden age. *Entertainment Weekly,* p. 7.

Jenson, R. (2013). Americans pick Ronald McDonald over Burger King for President. *Public Policy Polling.* Retrieved on March 24, 2020 at: https://www.publicpolicypolling.com/wp-content/uploads/2017/09/PPP_Release_NationalFOOD_022613.pdf.

Joyella, M. (2019, February 26). Rachel Maddow is No. 1 I February ratings, but so is Sean Hannity. *Forbes.* Retrieved on March 24, 2020 at: https://www.forbes.com/sites/markjoyella/2019/02/26/cable-news-ratings-rachel-maddow-is-no-1-and-so-is-sean-hannity/#73f85a997730.

Koszarski, R. (1990). *An evening's entertainment: The age of the silent feature picture, 1915–1928, Volume 3.* New York: Charles Scribner & Sons.

McCarthy, M. (2005, May 23). Burger King tries old slogan again. USA Today. Retrieved on March 24, 2020 at: https://usatoday30.usatoday.com/money/advertising/adtrack/2005-05-23-burger-king_x.htm.

Miller, W. (1959). *A canticle for Leibowitz.* Philadelphia, PA: J. B. Lippenscott and Company.

"Newspapers Fact Sheet" (2019, July 9). *Pew Research Center.* Retrieved at: https://www.journalism.org/fact-sheet/newspapers/.

Otterson, J. (2019, February 25). Oscars 2019 ratings rise from last year to 29.6 million viewers. *Variety.* Retrieved on March 24, 2020 at: https://variety.com/2019/tv/news/oscars-ratings-2019-1203144417/.

Panek, E., Hollenbach, C., Yang, J., & Rhodes, T. (2018). The effects of group size and time on the formation of online communities: Evidence from Reddit. *Social Media + Society,* 4(4). Retrieved on March 24, 2020 at: https://journals.sagepub.com/doi/full/10.1177/2056305118815908.

Porter, R. (2019a, February 6). TV ratings: 46.8 million watch State of the Union, up a little vs. 2018. *The Hollywood Reporter.* Retrieved on March 24, 2020 at: https://www.hollywoodreporter.com/live-feed/state-union-tv-ratings-tuesday-feb-5-2019-1183327.

Porter, R. (2019b, May 20). 'Game of Thrones' series finale sets all-time HBO ratings record. *The Hollywood Reporter.* Retrieved on March 24, 2020 at: https://www.hollywoodreporter.com/live-feed/game-thrones-series-finale-sets-all-time-hbo-ratings-record-1212269.

Prior, M. (2007). *Post-broadcast democracy: How media choice increases inequality in political involvement and polarizes elections.* Cambridge: Cambridge University Press.

Stafford, L. (2015, October 3). Hundreds turn out for first Chick-Fil-A store in New York. *The Atlanta Journal-Constitution.* Retrieved on March 24, 2020 at: https://www.ajc.com/business/hundreds-turnout-for-first-chick-fil-store-new-york/D1jv9mDWtZIsh2pXFTYsWK/.

Statista. (2016). Leading ad supported broadcast and cable networks in the United States in 2015, by average number of viewers. Accessed 11/11/16: https://www.statista.com/statistics/530119/tv-networks-viewers-usa/

Stelter, B. (2015, August 7). Fox's GOP debate had record 24 million viewers. *CNN*. Retrieved on March 24, 2020 at: http://money.cnn.com/2015/08/07/media/gop-debate-fox-news-ratings/.

"The Transformation of Network News" (1999, June 15). *Nieman Reports*. Retrieved on March 24, 2020 at: https://niemanreports.org/articles/the-transformation-of-network-news/.

Tolentino, J. (2019). *Trick mirror: Reflections on self delusion*. New York: Random House.

Watson, A. (2019, December 18). The most-watched TV episodes in the U.S. Statista. Retrieved on March 24, 2020 at: https://www.statista.com/statistics/665425/most-watched-tv-episodes-usa

Welch, A. (2019, June 18). Late night ratings: June 10–14, 2019: 'Kimmel' comes out on top. *TV by the Numbers*. Retrieved on March 24, 2020 at: https://tvbythenumbers.zap2it.com/weekly-ratings/late night-ratings-june-10-14-2019/.

When 'Mass' Meant 'Massive': Cohesive Audiences and Heavy Impact

One could argue that the pinnacle of mass media audience levels ascribed too much power to single entities—and sometimes even single persons. For instance, Walter Cronkite helmed the CBS Evening News for 19 years (1962–1981), with national polls frequently finding him to be the most trusted man in America (Folkenflik, 2009). When Cronkite offered his signature phrase at the end of each broadcast, "and that's the way it is," large swaths of the U.S. concurred. Allowing a single media figure to have such sway over a mass audience can certainly be concerning, yet most would agree Cronkite wore the crown of trust quite well.

However, Cronkite is a key exemplar for why mass communication is an extremely important field of inquiry to navigate both our past and present worlds. Both terms—"mass" and "communication"—are key components of this concept. "Communication" is a means of disseminating information, ideas, attitudes, and feelings to others (the audience) via messages (technically we would say it is a way to try to evoke meaning in audiences, rather than "transmission"). The size of the audience for a given message, of course, is an important factor in determining the magnitude of effects in communication. The larger the audience, the greater the potential for influence and reverberation (other factors, such as who is the intended audience, matter as well). Of course, some audience members will experience little or no influence from a given message—but those who did not see, hear, or read a message cannot possibly be affected directly by it. In contrast to the term "broadcasting" which still holds as it pertains to the ability to cast messages broadly, mass communication warrants reconsideration, as one cannot learn about a given audience before first assessing the size of that group.

At some point, a message with a large enough audience can be considered an instance of "mass" communication—there is no clear cutoff number for when an audience is large enough to be considered "mass" communication. Furthermore, one can look at the sheer size of the audience (numerical size) to be the appropriate yardstick; it is also possible to consider audience share (percentage of potential audience) as another way to measure audience size. As we will explain, the size of an audience is influenced by the medium concerned. Interpersonal or dyadic communication (e.g. one-on-one speech) happens repeatedly—literally billions of times every day—but each instance involves a very small audience. Many live public speeches can reach larger audiences than dyadic communication, but public speeches still have a relatively limited audience size unless they are broadcast. Books, followed by newspapers and magazines, increased the potential reach of a given message beyond those physically present at a speech. Electronic media, such as radio and television further extended the number of people who could be reached by a single message. The Internet—exemplified today as Twitter, Facebook, Instagram, and Amazon—increased exponentially the potential audience for messages. Note that we can now use more traditional media, such as newspapers or television, via the Internet.

The technology of a mass medium enables—and limits—communication. The printing press is one invention that can be said to have allowed mass communication: For the first time one message (a book, a pamphlet, a newspaper) could be read by many people, more than ever before possible. The advent of network radio and television expanded the size of the potential audience. Newspapers had large circulations but so many individual newspapers are published that the "newspaper audience" is split into many smaller groups. Then the birth of the Internet allowed messages to be disseminated to millions of people; however, it was fragmented like newspapers. Unlike other mass media advents, consumers were not limited by elements of reach, such as geography or mail delivery. Instead, users had many, many webpages to visit and could just as easily access information from thousands of miles away as something produced down the street. It is worth noting that the Internet combined *existing* media: A webpage could display print and photos like newspapers did, audio like radio and television, and video like television. This sounds basic when one considers it, yet we often still here misnomers about these concepts today. For example, when one indicates they do not need to consult newspapers or magazines anymore because they have Facebook and Twitter, one fails to acknowledge that neither of those social media platforms hires writers or journalists to advance regular news content. Rather, some of these same news structures as before are delivering the content via social media, albeit often without any print counterpart to its delivery mechanism.

The Internet also created the opportunity for email. Unfortunately for those who hate spam, some users quickly realized the potential for one email message to reach millions of people. Mass communication using this medium was limited only by the users list of email addresses for intended recipients, but quickly people realized the law of diminishing returns of emailed news content as one could triple the amount of news sent or forwarded, but rarely would get triple the readership in the process, as recipients learned how to cull content down to the most necessary and interesting. The more the amount of news proliferated, the more the percentage of news advanced went unread.

The proliferation of cable television, satellite, as well as Internet webpages and social media, allowed more people to receive messages than ever before. But, like newspapers, the multitude of channels spread the audience across many separate messages. As these other options grew, the domination of the core broadcast television networks declined. They still reached millions, but we observe that the percent of the population exposed to a given message diminished—dramatically so.

Population and Technology Escalate Potential Audience Size

Two major considerations—population growth and improvements in communication technology—have historically fueled growth in the size of audiences in mass communication. Research estimates the world population around 70,000 B.C. was between 1,000 and 10,000 people. 60,000 years later (around 10,000 B.C.), population had grown to between 1 and 15 million people. In the fourth century A.D., it had grown further to somewhere between 50 and 60 million. The world population reached the one billion milestone in about 1804. In 2020, the World Population Clock estimates indicate that 7.8 billion human beings inhabit this planet (2020). In the U.S. the Census counts the population every 10 years (Native Americans were not included in this count until 1860). The U.S. population grew from 350 in 1610 to 330 million in 2019 (U.S. Census Bureau, 2019). The population increased in every census or every ten years—without exception ("Demographic History," 2019). It is very clear that as the population around the world and in the U.S. grew over time, any given message had the potential to reach an increasingly larger audience. For example, according to the Census Bureau, in 1950 the population of the US was about 150 million, in order to reach 10 million people a given message must reach 15% of the population. Today, reaching an audience of 10 million viewers or readers requires only 3% of the population ("1950 United States Census," 2019).

The second key factor in the growth of the potential mass audience besides population growth is the emergence of new technologies. Initial technological advances occurred in other countries (e.g. papyrus in Egypt; the printing press with movable type in Germany). The development of paper (including papyrus) and the printing press allowed a message to reach more people than speech alone. It is estimated that before the advent of the printing press "finishing a single copy [of a book] could take weeks, even with long hours devoted only to writing" (Corwin, 2016). Rather than relying on monks to painstakingly copy books by hand, Johannes Gutenberg's invention of the printing press and movable type in 1439 allowed the mass production and dissemination of texts. A single text could be distributed to and read by large numbers of people. Introduction of the printing press had far-reaching implications for society and culture:

> In Renaissance Europe, the arrival of mechanical movable type printing introduced the era of mass communication, which permanently altered the structure of society. The relatively unrestricted circulation of information and (revolutionary) ideas transcended borders, captured the masses in the Reformation and threatened the power of political and religious authorities. The sharp increase in literacy broke the monopoly of the literate elite on education and learning and bolstered the emerging middle class. ("Printing Press," 2018)

This marvelous invention did have some limitations. The quotation presented above makes it clear that the utility of books is dependent on the literacy of the population, which was quite limited at the time of Gutenberg's invention. Second, books had to be purchased, meaning that the number of books in circulation was limited by disposable income. Furthermore, unlike broadcast television, a given book title typically does not reach the entire audience simultaneously; this factor (the fact that books do not simultaneously reach all readers) dilutes the reach of the message in a book to some extent, making modern outliers in this regard particularly noteworthy, such as when last book in the *Harry Potter* series sold 8.3 million copies on the day it was released (Rich, 2007). In fact, even with the gigantic reach of the *Bible*, no single book has ever reached every member of the potential audience. Still, the printing press meant that messages could be disseminated eventually to millions of readers.

At this point we turn our focus to the United States (although we believe our subsequent analysis is pertinent to other countries as well). The development of newspaper publishing further advanced the evolution of mass communication. Newspapers started publishing in the American colonies "in Boston in

1690 when Benjamin Harris published ... *Public Occurrences, both Foreign and Domestick*" (Baldasty, 1992, p. 137). Through 1900 newspapers had relatively small audiences: "Early in the [19th] century, newspapers were usually small in circulation, four-page weeklies or dailies" (p. 34). The number of daily newspapers soared to 2,042 in 1920 and by 1970, "78% of the adult population read a daily paper" (Baldasty, p. 137). McGarr (1986) reported that "The average circulation of daily papers climbed from 2,200 a day in 1840 to 8004 in 1904 and 16,684 in 1925" (p. 108); "by 1892 daily circulation had climbed to ... 374,000" (pp. 125–126). In fact, research established that in America newspaper circulation from 1920–1950 increased faster than the population (Hobsbawn, 1994, p. 194). We should keep in mind the fact that different newspapers offered readers different content; just as two books with different content do not disseminate the same message.

In colonial America, most papers were initially subsidized by political parties, resulting in "partisan content [that] dominated pre-Civil War American newspapers" (Baldasty, p. 7). Furthermore, at that time papers were limited to reporting the news and ideas its own staff had collected. Obviously, people could only learn the information reported in the newspaper they read, not the information that was reported in other newspapers. Information could spill from one paper to another, but a time lag in the dissemination of ideas was necessarily involved. It was also possible that a message circulated by the postal system could end up being published in more than one newspaper. Many larger cities had more than one newspaper; however, the number of cities with two or more daily newspapers fell from 579 in 1920 to 49 by 2001 (Baldasty, 1992, p. 147) which tended to concentrate newspaper audiences. The audience reach of a given news story was given a hefty boost with the formation of the Associated Press (AP) in 1846. The AP—and later its competitor United Press International (UPI)—collected stories and distributed them to member newspapers who could publish these articles. This meant that the ideas in a particular story could appear in multiple newspapers on the same day. Each paper could publish unique local news as well as wire released stories, but reliance on AP and UPI for content meant that many newspapers could offer the same content to their readers at the same time. This shift away from a multitude of daily newspapers to a smaller number of these outlets with larger audiences tended to homogenize audiences—yet often without the audience realizing the homogenization was occurring. Most read the local paper with the same local gaze, even when the story originated from an AP or UPI writer whose intended audience was anyone in America with access to a newspaper.

First radio, and then television, provided new means of reaching audiences beyond books, newspapers, and magazines (we discuss the Internet and social media later). Radio station 9XM (University of Wisconsin, now known as WHA) broadcast music in 1917 and speech in 1921. The more widely known station

KDKA began broadcasts in Pittsburgh, PA, in 1920. The first news program was broadcast on radio in 1920 by the station 8MK, now called WWJ ("History of Radio," 2018). By 2006 the U.S. had over 13,000 radio stations (Noam, 2009). The rise of broadcasting networks enabled a particular message to reach increasingly larger audiences. The NBC radio network started regular programming in 1924 (Gunther, 1999). CBS began sending network programs to stations in 1927 (Gunther, 1999). AP began distributing its news stories to radio stations in 1941 (Associated Press, 2018). Radio had developed large audiences and network programming increased the homogeneity of the content of these broadcasts, effectively enlarging the audience for a many stories.

The Federal Communications Commission (FCC) first issued commercial television licenses in 1941 (Quartz, 2018). NBC and CBS began broadcasting television news in the late 1940s. In 1963 the *Huntley-Brinkley Report* expanded from 15 to 30 minutes (Gunther, 1999). AP started distributing video programming to TV stations in 1994 (Associated Press, 2018), meaning that some of the same stories and the information therein became available to newspapers, radio stations, and television stations. By 2016, AP news was used by over 1,300 newspapers and broadcasters. The greater the reliance on a common source of stories, the more homogeneous the content of mass media and the common fund of knowledge held by people increased as this occurred.

At this point it becomes necessary to refine our definition of "mass communication." The definition from the *Cambridge Dictionary* (2018) serves our purpose, stipulating that mass communication refers to messages that reach a large audience at (roughly) the same time: Mass communication is "something such as television or the Internet that means that a message, story, etc. can be communicated to a large number of people at the same time." Books as a medium have the limitation that not every member of the audience reads a book at the same time or at the same pace (and, of course, that a given book reaches a limited number of readers). Some overlap in readership is present, but each individual book reaches a different audience (with different content). Newspapers, particularly at first, had the limitation that the content of each newspaper differed, so that comparatively small audiences consumed a single message. However, the advent of radio and television (and AP and UPI) meant that stories heard or seen by their audience at the essentially the same time. Even more interestingly, these outlets (along with many others) often would have multiple versions of the same article: one to break the news, one to add details as the stories develop, and one for the historic archive.

We want to explicitly indicate that in this conceptualization, it is the specific message—not the medium—that determines whether a message should be considered an instance of mass communication. That is, two different books, or two different television programs, or two different movies do not qualify as "mass communication." Only when the same message is consumed by the members of an audience should communication truly be considered mass communication. The proverb about whether a tree falling in the forest makes a sound is relevant here: without readers, watchers, or listeners, a message has no influence.

It may sound counter-intuitive, but by our conceptualization, communication via the telephone is not an instance of mass communication. It is true that millions and millions of people are connected by telephones but, for the most part, a conversation connects two people at a time. This fact is not a limitation of email, with which one spam message could reach millions of users. Even considering conference calls the size of the audience for any given message communicated by telephone is very small. We must acknowledge an annoying exception: the obnoxious "robo-call," in which a single recorded message reaches many people at more or less the same time.

For us the apex of mass communication occurred when the three major broadcast networks dominated communication. In the mid-1970s, according to David Poltrack, executive vice president for research at CBS, "'when viewers turned on the TV set, they had five choices [ABC, CBS, NBC, PBS and an independent local station], and the networks were three of them.' At the time the three-network share of audience hovered around 90%" (Lowry, 1997; see also Arceneaux & Johnson, 2013). Notice that with such high market penetration even a program in third place in the ratings could qualify as an instance of mass communication. Similarly, Prior (2007) indicated that in 1970 network "television was universally available .... The three broadcast networks and their affiliates dominated television, capturing 80% of all viewing .... Of those who had their televisions on, three-quarters watched one of the network news programs" (p. 1). Gunther (1999) reported that the situation concerning the three broadcast networks shifted over time:

> During 1998, the three evening newscasts reached a combined average of about 30.4 million viewers in 22 million homes. This represents a reach that is greater than the total circulation of the nation's 10 largest newspapers. Prime-time news programs connect with even larger audiences. CBS's "60 Minutes" (Sunday), the industry leader, has attracted an average of 13.4 million homes so far during the 1998–99 TV season. And "60 Minutes" is only one of 14 prime-time, hour-long news shows appearing on the Big Three.

Particularly when one considers the percentage of the population who were exposed to the same message, network television programming embodied the concept of mass communication as a message from one person or content source to many people.

In the era dominated by broadcast television, most people shared much the same fund of knowledge. Williams and Delli Carpini (2011) explained that "for the first time in history people unknown to each other who met knew what each had in all probability heard (or later, seen) the night before: The big game, the favorite comedy show, Winston Churchill's speech, the contents of the news bulletin" (p. 51). In popular culture, this phenomenon is sometimes referred to as a "watercooler show," which we will explore more directly in Chapter 6. The three major broadcast (ABC, CBS, and NBC) networks in the 1970's, 1980's and 1990's offered relatively similar news, in sharp contrast to, for example, cable networks CNN and FOX News today. Stelter (2012) observed that "For decades, there were only 'marginal differences' among NBC, ABC and CBS .... Each of the Big Three nightly newscasts on American television tended to open with the same story— the latest campaign speech, a new government study, or perhaps a big snowstorm." Selecting which newscast to view was largely about the anchor and feel of the show, yet rarely about what content would be shown—or the valence infused within that content. Arceneaux and Johnson (2013) concur, explaining that "in the 1970s ... the news shows for on these networks [ABC, CBS, NBC] were nearly identical" (p. 5), at times using the same video footage for expediency and economic factors. In fact, research established that "over the first two decades of television history, program diversity declined" (Dimmick, 2010; see also Dominick & Pearce, 1976 and Wakshlag & Adams, 1985). So, we argue that mass communication reached its apex in the broadcast era when a large percent of the public consumed roughly the same information creating shared knowledge about the world and people and events in it.

Fragmenting Entertainment: Sports and Scripted Content Targeted with Pinpoint Accuracy

News, of course, was no anomaly. The Internet fragmented in ways that were delightful in the boundaries they razed (e.g. allowing the aging Florida snowbird from New York the chance to read the local newspaper and watch the Knicks play) as well as the options they provided (e.g. allowing a struggling musician access to fans it previous had to busk streets to find, reducing the distribution costs that previously hindered aspiring filmmakers). The byproduct of all of that innovation, though, was the lack of a commonly embraced (or at least acknowledged) center of the media universe.

Nowhere was this felt more than in sports media. Some products seemed relatively immune from the fragmentation (NFL football, for instance, still was a once-a-week sport where games overlapped with others, creating Sunday as focused media consumption days), yet the large majority of products felt the influence. No sport exemplifies this effect more than baseball. With 162 regular season games plus a month of post-season contests, baseball's inventory was massive, yet little of it reached mass media. In the 1970s and early 1980s, there was a Saturday game of the week and, for brief stints of time, ABC's *Monday Night Baseball*, which became *Sunday Afternoon Baseball* (Walker & Bellamy, 2008). Two games per week were advanced to content-starved fans with these contests rarely involving those fans' favorite teams. The World Series, dubbed the "Fall Classic" was such a contrast that mass audiences would tune in. Nielsen Media Research (2007) reported the peak of all World Series viewership occurred in 1978, when 44.3 million Americans tuned in. Most games had limited audiences.

Then came cable, with Atlanta's SuperStation showing Braves games and WGN's Chicago Channel 9 showing Cubs baseball on a near-daily basis. This was followed by ESPN's baseball contract that showed baseball on the majority of the days of the week (Walker & Bellamy, 2008). Then the Internet, MLB Network, and speciality packages such as MLB Extra Innings finished the mass baseball audience, allowing out-of-market fans virtual unlimited access. Baseball was now plentiful in media (which raised baseball's coffers considerably, to a record $10.3B in 2018; Brown, 2019) yet lowered the rarity of events like the World Series, which plunged in ratings to just 13.9 million in 2019 (Paulsen, 2019).

Other sports follow similar paths, albeit with different relative peaks. The NBA peaked with Jordan-era Bulls teams but now has similar ubiquity that heightens profits but lowers Finals ratings. Advents like The Tennis Channel or the Motor Racing Network deplete ratings for Wimbledon or the Daytona 500.

Non-sports entertainment has these types of peaks and then dispersions, too, as will be covered in greater detail later in this book (particularly in Chapter 3). As you read, similar patterns will emerge—peak music album buys were in the late 1970s; peak network scripted television was the mid-1980s. Population growth and inflation hide much of these trends. For instance, a quick glance at box office receipts would tell you that going to the movie theater has never been more popular, with over $11B in receipts each of the past two years (2018 and 2019). Such figures seemingly dwarf the $1.26B in receipts in 1982, yet consider the contrast and one gets a different story. 2018, for instance, had $11.8B in total gross, but featured 921 films offered to a population of 330 million Americans at an average movie ticket rate of $9.11; meanwhile, 1982 had $1.26B in total gross from just 69 films to a population of 231 million at an average movie ticket rate of $2.94 ("Domestic Yearly Box Office", 2019; *Suneson*, 2019). In the end, the case becomes murky and we realize that while the majority of Americans used to regularly attend films each year, 46% of Americans now go one time or less per year (Watson, 2019). Ask your family-owned theater when the golden days were and you will likely hear answers about the pre-Internet era.

Conclusion

The "mass" that is no longer there is the theme of this chapter and the context for the rest of this book. We work to avoid value judgments on whether new media ecologies are "better" or "worse" than prior iterations, yet for one to study media change, one must first acknowledge the change in media. We have seen that population growth continuously increased the potential size of the audience for communication. For centuries, technological innovations spurred the increase of audience size but recent technological advances—particularly social media—fragmented audiences into smaller and smaller groups. The audience for the three major networks in the 1970s, the apex of mass audiences, splintered apart as many smaller groups of people watched different messages in a variety of media. Furthermore, for television viewing, cable TV, satellite TV, Netflix, Prime video (Amazon) further divide the audience. For music, iTunes, Spotify, and Pandora can siphon off part of the potential mass audience. No matter the device or form of media, a splintering has occurred. We will devote the next two chapters to this splintering that we dub media balkanization, applying the concepts to news (Chapter 2) and entertainment (Chapter 3) in equal measure.

References

1950 United States Census. (2019). Wikipedia. Accessed 8/20/19: https://en.wikipedia.org/wiki/1950_United_States_Census.

Arceneaux, K., & Johnson, M. (2013). *Changing minds or changing channels: Media effects in the era of expanded choice.* Chicago: University of Chicago Press.

Associated Press. (2018). Wikipedia. Accessed 12/22/18: https://en.wikipedia.org/wiki/Associated_Press.

Baldasty, G. J. (1992). *The commercialization of news in the nineteenth century.* Madison, WI: University of Wisconsin Press.

Brown, M. (2019, January 7). MLB sees record revenues of $10.3 Billion for 2018. *Forbes.* Retrieved March 24, 2020 at: https://www.forbes.com/sites/maurybrown/2019/01/07/mlb-sees-record-revenues-of-10-3-billion-for-2018/#54742c6c5bea.

Cambridge Dictionary. (2018). Mass communication. Accessed 12/22/18: http://dictionary.cambridge.org/us/dictionary/english/mass-communication".

Corwin, V. (2016). Medieval book production and monastic life. Dartmouth Ancient Books Lab. Accessed 3/27/20: https://sites.dartmouth.edu/ancientbooks/2016/05/24/medieval-book-production-and-monastic-life/.

Demographic History of the United States: Historical Census Population. (2019). Wikipedia. Accessed 7/9/19: https://en.wikipedia.org/wiki/Demographic_history_of_the_United_States.

Dimmick, J. W. (2010). *Media competition and coexistence*. London: Routledge.

"Domestic Yearly Box Office". (2019). Box Office Mojo. Retrieved at: https://www.boxofficemojo.com/year/.

Dominick, J. R., & Pearce, M. C. (1976). Trends in network prime-time programming, 1953–1964. *Journal of Communication, 20*, 70–80.

Folkenflik, D. (2009, July 18). Walter Cronkite, America's "most trusted man", dead. NPR. Retrieved at: https://www.npr.org/templates/story/story.php?storyId=106770499.

Gunther, M. (1999, June 15). The transformation of network news. *Nieman Reports*. Accessed 11/11/16: http://niemanreports.org/articles/the-transformation-of-network-news/.

History of Radio. (2018). Wikipedia Accessed 12/22/18: https://en.wikipedia.org/wiki/History_of_radio).

Hobsbawn, E. (1994). *The age of extremes: A history of the world, 1914–1991*. New York: Pantheon Books.

Knapton, S. (2016, January 20). Facebook users have 155 friends. *Telegraph*. Accessed 2/17/17: http://www.telegraph.co.uk/news/science/science-news/12108412/Facebook-users-have-155-friends-but-would-trust-just-four-in-a-crisis.html.

Lowry, B. (1997, September 2). Cable stations gather strength. *LA Times*. Accessed 12/12/16: http://articles.latimes.com/1997/sep/02/entertainment/ca-28033.

McGarr, M. E. (1986). *The decline of popular politics*. New York: Oxford University Press.

Nielsen Media Research. (2007). MLB World Series. Retrieved at: http://blog.nielsen.com/nielsenwire/wp-content/uploads/2008/10/pr_mlb_worldseries_yearthru07.xls.

Noam, E. M. (2009). *Media ownership and concentration in America*. Oxford: University Press.

Paulsen. (2019). Game 7 helps World Series avoid all-time lows. *Sports Media Watch*. Retrieved at: https://www.sportsmediawatch.com/2019/10/world-series-ratings-second-lowest-nationals-astros-fox/.

Printing Press. (2018). Wikipedia. Accessed 12/22/18: https://en.wikipedia.org/wiki/Printing_press.

Prior, M. (2007). *Post-broadcast democracy: How media choice increases inequality in political involvement and polarizes elections*. Cambridge: Cambridge University Press.

Quartz. (2018). Watch: The first TV commercial, which aired 75 years ago today. *Wikipedia*. Accessed 12/22/18: https://qz.com/721431/watch-the-first-tv-commercial-which-aired-75-years-ago-today/.

Rich, M. (2007, July 22). Record first-day sales for last "Harry Potter book." *New York Times*. Accessed 8/20/19: https://www.nytimes.com/2007/07/22/books/22cnd-potter.html.

Statista. (2016). Leading ad supported broadcast and cable networks in the United States in 2015, by average number of viewers. Accessed 11/11/16: https://www.statista.com/statistics/530119/tv-networks-viewers-usa/seebmpC:\b\RiseFallMassComm\tv-networks-viewers-usa-.

Statista.(2019).Twitter: Number of monthly active U.S. users 2010–2019, Accessed 6/6/19: https://www.statista.com/statistics/274564/monthly-active-twitter-users-in-the-united-states/.

Stelter, B. (2012, January 8). Big three newscasts are changing the state of play. *New York Times*. Accessed 1/4/19: https://www.nytimes.com/2012/01/09/business/media/at-abc-cbs-and-nbc-news-accentuating-the-differences.html?pagewanted=all.

Stelter, B. (2015, August 7). FOX's GOP debate had record 24 million viewers. *CNN*. Accessed 6/15/16: http://money.cnn.com/2015/08/07/media/gop-debate-fox-news-ratings/.

Stewart, P. A., Eubanks, A. D., & Miller, J. (2019). Visual priming and framing of the 2016 GOP and Democratic Party presidential primary debates. *Politics and the Life Sciences, 38*, 14–31.

Suneson, G. (2019, August 29). From pocket change to nearly $10: The cost of the movie ticket the year you were born. *USA Today*. Accessed 3/27/20: https://www.usatoday.com/story/money/2019/08/29/cost-of-a-movie-ticket-the-year-you-were-born/39998123/.

U.S. Census Bureau. (2019). U.S. and world population clock. Accessed 3/27/20: https://www.census.gov/popclock/.

Wakshlag, J., & Adams, W. (1985). Trends in programming variety and the prime-time access rule. *Journal of Broadcasting and Electronic Media, 29*, 23–34.

Walker, J. R., & Bellamy, R. V. (2008). *Center field shot: A history of baseball on television*. Lincoln, NE: University of Nebraska Press.

Watson, A. (2019, August 27). Frequency of going to movie theaters to see a movie among adults in the United States as of June 2019. *Statista*. Retrieved at: https://www.statista.com/statistics/264396/frequency-of-going-to-the-movies-in-the-us/.

Williams, B. A., & Delli Carpini, M. X. (2011). *After broadcast news: Media regimes, democracy, and the new media environment*. Cambridge: University Press.

World Population Clock. (2020). Worldometer. Accessed 2/4/20: https://www.worldometers.info/world-population/.

CHAPTER TWO

Partisan, Hostile, Fake, or Real: The Fragmentation of News

In late 2019, two concurrent narratives played out in political media. One featured hearings for the impeachment of Republican President Donald J. Trump; the other unfolded quite differently on social media and in other conservative outlets. For instance, in one world, Democratic House Speaker Nancy Pelosi announced Congress would advance impeachment charges against Trump "with the utmost gravity" while in the other world, four minutes after Pelosi was done speaking, President Trump used Twitter to call the decision "witch hunt garbage" and then, 30 *seconds* after that, Trump's re-election campaign, grabbed the President's baton. Although most mainstream media outlets relayed the gravity of the impeachment charges, Bennett and Wilson (2019) document that 20 minutes (and just $100,000) was all it took to place paid advertisements in the feeds of two million Facebook accounts, each exclaiming that "The ONLY thing stopping Democrats from carrying out their impeachment WITCH HUNT is Patriotic Americans standing with President Trump" (emphasis original, p. 52). The campaign message then filters through Facebook and becomes less easily traced; once one of those two million people shared the ad, it still appeared as Trump-sponsored on the user/ sharer's account, yet conspicuously does not get presented as Trump-sponsored to accounts in which the content is shared. Suddenly, it appears in tens of millions of other feeds, everyone is producing "witch hunt"-related messages. Americans were talking about the same topic, but the postulates we typically tout via agenda-setting theory (McCombs & Shaw, 1972) have been inordinately altered depending on which reality one accepts.

Of course, we say these were two concurrent narratives, but the truth is that those story-lines quickly fragmented into millions. Some narratives combined the legitimacy of the impeachment narrative with a cocktail of CNN and a social media feed urging support for Joe Biden or lamenting the calamity of climate change while quoting activist child Greta Thunberg. For others, the cocktail could perhaps combine Rush Limbaugh rhetoric with social media feeds persuading people to buy Donald Trump Jr.'s book or criticizing the people saying "Happy Holidays" instead of "Merry Christmas." Feeds are exactly what they claim to be: personalized, customized, and designed to give each person more of what they might "like." News is offered in intermittent, short bursts, each in a unique combination along with a feed that might feature a Chicago Bears meme, a picture of the meal a childhood friend was having at the moment, or a coworker announcing a major life change. The clutter amalgamates news as part of a larger ecosystem, each as unique as a snowflake.

It was not always this way. Past audiences were massive but now audiences can be split in many ways; as such, this chapter takes up seven news-related balkanization topics. It begins by establishing that the mass media in America (likely elsewhere) has fragmented into smaller and smaller audiences. It then discusses the impact of the FCC's (Federal Communication Commission) retraction of the Fairness Doctrine. We document the rise of ideological polarization in America. Next, we argue that rhetoric (communication) is epistemic (messages create our world view or knowledge). We note that the nature of information available from messages varies by content source. The process of processing messages is elucidated next. Finally, we address the recent attacks on "fake news." Throughout these seven topics, we seek to focus on ideological divisions in audiences. Again, we do not argue that there is zero overlap in audience members between audiences, only that different audiences can have very different patterns or emphasizes of media use (media diets) which expose them to different information and/or entertainment.

Gradual Fragmentation of the Mass Media Audience

In the not too distant past, many messages have attracted large audiences as would be expected in an era of mass communication. For example, President Nixon's resignation speech attracted an audience of 128 million. The Commission on Presidential Debates reports that the first Nixon-Kennedy debate on September 26, 1960 drew 66.4 million viewers, which was 36.7% of the U.S. population. People watched the same scripted programs to the point that one of those programs could legitimately claim to be the *Battle of the Network Stars* (1976–1988)—because most of the stars were, indeed, recognized and known by the general public. Mass media messages reached millions of viewers.

Today, however, far fewer media events attract that many viewers. For instance, Fox's first 2016 GOP primary debate was watched by only 24 million people (even though this was the most-watched presidential primary debate in history; Stelter, 2015), representing about 7% of the populace at the time. Mark (2019) reported that about 13 million people watched the first day of the Trump impeachment hearings in the House. The first day of the Senate trial attracted the attention of about 11 million people (Farhi, 2020). James Comey's (former FBI Director) testimony and Brett Kavanaugh's Senate appearance were watched by about 20 million people. These messages from Comey and Kavanaugh each constituted about 6% of the population. Huge audiences—especially when considered as a percent of the potential audience—are far less common today than in the past. The decreasing size of audiences for content sources (and concomitant increase in the number of diverse audiences) cannot help but dilute the potential influence of these content sources. We operationalize "content sources" at various levels of abstraction, to include news media generally, particular networks, or individual broadcasts. Similarly this phrase encompasses social media generally, more specific social media (such as Twitter and Facebook), and particular Twitter feeds or Facebook pages. Content sources can include newspapers generally or specific newspapers. They can include broadcasts of sports such as soccer, baseball, tennis, or football or the broadcasts of particular games. Content sources can include types of entertainment such as movies, concerts, as well as TV dramas and comedies. It can refer to genres of movies or television shows or a specific movie or TV series or a specific episode. These sources all offer some form of content or message to an audience.

It is possible to segment audiences in a variety of ways, with each possible grouping splitting the potential audience into smaller slices. One could separate audiences by age (surely people of different ages do not have identical media diets); other possible divisions can be found in socio-economic status, gender orientation, ethnicity, or education level. We do not argue that there is no overlap, for example, between people who attended a college or university and those who stopped their formal education after high school (or before). But surely each group has a different constellation of media consumed (the felicitous word "constellation" is adopted from Campbell & Jamieson [1978], who use it in their definition of genres of rhetoric). Similarly, people vary in their interest in sports generally and in specific sports. Millions watch the NFL; millions (again, with some overlap) follow NCAA basketball. Many people have watched movies from the Marvel

Universe; others consume Star Wars movies (Bill, for example, has watched all the Star Wars movies but none of the Marvel films while Andrew has seen the majority of Marvel films but has yet to complete a *Game of Thrones* episode).

For years people were limited to three viewing options—ABC, NBC, CBS—and perhaps a blurry PBS station as, before cable TV, television was broadcast and some stations were less powerful than others, reducing the quality of images for some viewers. For example, when the Nixon-Kennedy debates occurred in 1960, if you wanted to watch television while a debate was in progress you had no choice but to watch the debate: These important political events appeared on all of the networks; no other viewing options were available on television during the debates. Because the content was mostly constant across networks (e.g. all networks covered the same debate and, for a time, presidential debates had only one camera feed for all networks). At that time there were no VCR's or DVD players, no Internet, no satellite or cable TV. As time progressed, technology began to introduce other options for attracting viewers' attention such as VHS (and Betamax; both invented in Japan but quickly introduced in the U.S.) and DVR recording.

Cable TV brought dozens and then hundreds of channels to audiences. Commercial cable television began in the 1950s and peaked in 2000 at about 69 million subscribers ("Cable Television," 2020). Satellite TV, introduced in 1974 ("Satellite Television," 2020) provided further to the options for viewers. The Internet exploded with a myriad of other things to watch, listen to, or read; the Internet also made social media possible. Unlike the golden age of broadcast television, today those who are uninterested in politics have many other viewing options if they do not wish to watch debates. These technological advances provided viewers with choices, which reduced the size of the audience for a give message (including campaign messages). As communication technology advanced beyond the heyday of broadcast television, the mass audience began to fragment, a trend that has increased exponentially in recent years. Consider that hundreds of years passed between the invention of the printing press and the creating of newspapers. Radio and television rose to challenge newspapers as providers of information to the masses, followed by cable television and satellite TV. The introduction of the Internet rapidly unleashed countless webpages and made the ascendency of social media today a reality. As the Internet rose and moved into mainstream territory at the turn of the century, the ramifications seemed relatively rosy with implications benign. Tolentino (2019) writes of the late 1990s as the *You've Got Mail* era, "when it seemed that the very worst thing that could happen online was that you might fall in love with your business rival" (p. 2). However, understanding the impact of the Internet was difficult to grasp as balkanization had begun.

As the viewing options available to audience members increased—with the growth of VCRs, DVD players, cable TV, satellite TV, and the Internet, including social media—the percentage of the population who watched the nightly news and events such as debates dropped. Some people are political "junkies," who seek out at much information as possible, but many others were happy to take advantage of alternative programming when choices became available.

When a new content source emerges—for example, when ABC, CBS, and NBC were joined by Fox News or MSNBC—the developers of the new content source must decide what content to offer. One route that could be taken is to try to duplicate existing content (ABC, CBS, NBC); another option is to offer different kinds of programming. Many new outlets chose the latter strategy, developing niche content (see, e.g. Dimmick, 2000). Fox News illustrates the path of offering contrasting content (programming informed by a conflicting ideology) to create a niche medium. Developing niche content sources is not necessarily a bad choice for profitability: Content sources with focused (niche) content are likely to attract a particular group of consumers. This means that advertisers who consider the content sources' users their target audience can take advantage of the niche content, which is meant to attract a niche audience. Advertising on more general content sources usually means that some advertising dollars are wasted, for example, touting make-up products to male viewers or advertising beard oil to women (some advertising is still wasted in niche information sources, but less). So, proliferation of media has a tendency to create heterogeneous content sources. As new content sources arise, audience members can self-select into a variety of relatively homogeneous audience groups. To some extent this is a recursive process as a content source continuously focuses content to attract a target audience and the target audience increases consumption of the niche information source.

Today, media consumers have an incredible array of sources to consume, some with different content. Statista (2016) reports network viewers between December 29, 2014 through November 29, 2016. Table 2.1 shows six frequently-watched networks divided along with the percentage of the American audience

Table 2.1: Ratings and Population Shares (2019). Source: Schneider, 2019

Network	Audience (millions)	% of U.S. Population
CBS	7.1	2.2
NBC	6.3	1.9
ABC	5.2	1.6
FOX	4.6	1.4
MSNBC	1.7	0.5
CNN	1	0.3
TOTAL	25.9	7.9

tuning in using 330 million people as the current American population (U.S. Census Bureau, 2019). Recall from the previous chapter that in the mid-1970s "the three-network share of audience hovered around 90%" (Lowry, 1997; see also Prior, 2006). In 2016, even including three new networks, network programming was consumed by less than 10% of the populace. So, network broadcast television use has been declining as other options opened up and the "mass" in "mass communication" has continued to shrink.

The rise of social media further splinted or fragmented the viewing audience. Consider two prominent social media, Facebook and Twitter. In 2018, Facebook enjoyed 205 million monthly active Facebook users in the United States. In the United States alone 68 million people used Twitter at least monthly in 2019; worldwide 330 million people use Twitter monthly (Statista, 2019). These are obviously huge audiences. However, the human attention span (and processing ability) has not increased substantially (see, e.g. Benoit & Holbert, 2010; Miller, 1956). There is still only so much information to which we can attend and process, it is simply not possible for a person to continue to watch as much network TV as in the past *and* add consumption of the Internet, other networks, and social media. As Prior (2007) noted, "at any given time television viewers must commit to one particular program. They can watch either entertainment or news, but not both" (p. 103; but see our comments below on dual screening). People have no alternative but to choose among the available content sources when they consume media messages. In the 1950s the advent of television reduced (but did not eliminate) the use of radio (Prior, 2007). Note again that we do not argue that there is zero overlap in audience members between niche audiences, only that different audiences can have very different constellations (patterns or emphasizes) of media use.

Some people do have huge followings on social media. For example, Portuguese soccer player Cristiano Ronaldo is at this time the most-liked person on Facebook, with over 120 million followers ("List of most-liked," 2019). The most followed Twitter account at the time belonged to singer Katy Perry (about 107 million followers; Statista, 2019). Although some of these followers are fake or bots as we will discuss in more depth within Chapter 5, it is clear that messages from these two people—and others—are clear examples of mass communication. However, overall Facebook pages have an average of 155 friends (Knapton, 2016); Twitter feeds have an average of 208 followers (Beevolve, 2017). Thus, the universe of Facebook and Twitter users are splintered into many, many smaller audiences. Some social media messages should be considered mass communication but many do not quality as mass media in our conceptualization. Notice that some followers of a given twitter feed could consume other media as well. If, for example, some of these followers watch CNN while others choose FOX, these choices fragment these audiences further.

It is important to realize that these fractured audiences are not random (or representative) subgroups of the entire population but have distinct characteristics. For example, examining viewership of the first six Democratic and first six Republican primary debates in 2016, Nielsen (2016) reported that "about 30.2 million viewers watched only the Democratic debates while roughly 29.2 million viewers only viewed the Republican debates. Additionally, 37.8 million viewers watched both debates." This means that viewers for these messages can be meaningfully divided into three groups—30 million people who watched the Democratic debates, 29 million citizens who watched Republican debates, and 38 million others who watched both groups of debates. So, these campaign messages (televised primary debates) split the electorate into three groups who received different messages by and about the candidates. As each of these three groups of voters used various combinations of other media (in addition to primary debates) such as newspapers, network news, or social media (and learning can arise from entertainment programming, such as late night shows; see, for example, Benoit & Glantz, 2017), these three audiences were further fragmented into smaller and smaller groups, each of which consumed a different group of content sources of information about the candidates. By definition, those who consume a niche information source have different interests from those who use other niche sources.

The FCC's Fairness Doctrine

An important factor here that we believe has gone relatively unnoticed is the elimination of the "Fairness Doctrine." The Federal Communication Commission had promulgated this rule in 1949, requiring that broadcast stations present contrasting views on controversial issues. Hemmer (2014) noted that "Conservatives felt the Fairness Doctrine unfairly tilted the playing field against them .... To conservatives, avoiding controversy inevitably meant silencing right-wing voices." The FCC revoked the Fairness Doctrine in August of 1987 during President Ronald Reagan's second term in office (Matthews, 2011), a decision that was upheld in court (Gill, 2016). The consequences of this action were seen quickly, as Rush Limbaugh's radio program became syndicated in 1988. Tucker (2017) argued that in the absence of the Fairness Doctrine, "talk-radio stations across the country soon began to run right-wing agitprop from dawn to dusk, flooding the public airwaves with shameless demonization of Democrats and progressives." This rule change also unshackles liberal programming. "By the time [Roger] Ailes entered the game, the American right had spent a generation seeking out conservative alternatives to the 'liberal media,' and America's news media was already in the midst of a revolution that made Fox News possible" (Hemmer, 2014).

There can be no doubt that the content of network news has changed drastically following the repeal of the Fairness Doctrine. It is clear, for example, that Fox News and CNN cover different topics and offer contrasting perspectives when they do cover the same topic. Broadcasters were then free to offer a single (slanted) perspective on current events without even appearing to provide balanced coverage of controversial topics. Today webpages, Twitter feeds, and Facebook pages have no legal reason to present every side of an issue (some may offer more than one side to a topic, but they are not *required* to do so). This change enabled a wide range of content options (media menus) for people to choose from and consume.

In short, we have seen that population growth continuously increased the potential size of the audience for communication. Furthermore, for centuries, technological innovations in communication spurred the increase of audience size. Williams and Delli Carpini observed that "At the height of the Age of Broadcast News each of the three dominant networks broadcast similar programming designed to attract the largest audience possible" (2011, p. 78). However, recent technological advances—particularly cable television, the Internet, and social media—have fragmented audiences into smaller and smaller heterogeneous groups which are consuming different content sources and therefore acquiring different information. The audience for the three major networks in the 1970s, the apex of mass audiences (particularly in terms of percentage of total population), splintered apart as many smaller groups of people watched different messages in a variety of media.

Consider the differences, for example, in the content of CNN and Fox News (below we address the differences in content from various media). The once "mass" media have become balkanized into a myriad of media with smaller audiences by the emergence of alternative media and FCC rule changes. We use the term "balkanization" as a metaphor for changes in mass media audiences (we develop implications in Chapter 8). *Wikipedia* notes that this term began as "is a geopolitical term for the process of fragmentation or division of a region or state into smaller regions or states that are often hostile or uncooperative with one another" ("Balkanization," 2019). This term aptly describes the current state of media: Audiences are splinted into smaller fragments, some of which are hostile to one another by design (think of CNN or MSNBC versus FOX). Choosing which content source to consume is guided, at least in part, on the desires of each individual viewer.

Uses and Gratifications Theory

Prior (2007) pointed out that "when alternatives arise, people have more choice, and their own motivations for watching become more important in predicting their viewing behavior" (p. 94). Greater choice also "reduces the homogenizing impact of the media environment" (p. 98). Uses and gratifications (U&G) theory is an important perspective for understanding media consumption. Rather than focus on the effects of media on users, U&G focuses attention on why people consume media. What does the audience get out of using media? Katz, Blumler, and Gurevitch (1973) outline the assumptions of this approach. U&G conceptualizes the audience as an active participant in communication, not just as a passive receiver. People associate media with desired functionality (the uses and/or gratifications they seek). Content sources (media) compete for audience based on how well they satisfy audience uses and gratifications. In other words, everyone has needs or desires that can be achieved (at least in part) by media consumption.

Several lists of the uses of, and gratifications from, mass media have been identified. McQuail, Blumler, and Brown (1972), for example, identify four uses. People use the mass media for entertainment or diversion. It should be obvious that a great deal of the mass media (drama, comedy, sports, music) provide entertainment to users and allow them to escape their stress. Second, mass media can help people develop personal relationships, enhancing their social interaction. A third use is to help develop an individual's personal identity. Finally, they discuss surveillance as a use, allowing them to become informed about the world, people, and things in the world (Leung, 2013, identifies five uses of social media, with much overlap with McQuail, Blumler, and Brown's 1972 list).

In the golden age of broadcast television, people had very few choices in mass media. However, as media balkanized, content sources (particularly new ones) vied to attract an audience. They made media choices based in part on the uses and gratifications they provided to their audience (U&G is not the only explanation for media choice; for example, people who do not have Internet access—less common today than in the recent past—simply cannot use that medium). So, when Fox News was born, it chose to provide a conservative viewpoint and attracted conservative viewers away from the networks they had consumed before. Of course, a variety of sports media emerged and competed to attract athletic supporters. We believe that technological innovations—particularly the Internet and social media—balkanized mass media into a myriad of nice content sources. Some of these content sources appealed to conservatives, some appealed to liberals. Viewers chose to consume media that they believed would satisfy their needs and provide gratifications.

The situation is more complicated than we have suggested. Both Democrats and Republicans use the news media for surveillance—learning about the world, people, objects, and events. However, citizens' ideology also shapes media choice. We could make similar observations, for example, about how some people seek media which appear to display ones preferred gender perspective (female, male, or gay/lesbian/bisexual/transgender perspectives). Similarly, people often seek entertainment, but they may prefer drama, or comedy, or documentaries. Uses and gratifications help explain media choice in a balkanized media environment but it is not the only variable influencing media choice (nor does this theory claim to do so).

Ideological Polarization in America

American voters have become increasingly polarized by ideology (the labels "liberal" and "conservative" do not translate completely to "Democrat" and "Republican," but we bracket these distinctions here). Prior (2007) reported that "American voters are more partisan today than three decades ago" (p. 245). Abramowitz (2018) reports that in recent years "a growing number of Americans have been voting against the opposing party rather than for their own party" (p. 5). This pattern has become more pronounced in the last 20 years. Ideological polarization is particularly marked among citizens who vote in elections (Prior, 2007). Sabato, Kondik and Skelley (2016) noted that in the 2016 elections every state that voted for Donald Trump elected a Republican senator while every state that voted for Hillary Clinton elected a Democratic senator. Abramowitz and Webster (2016) observed that "Recent elections in the United States have been characterized by the highest levels of party loyalty and straight-ticket voting since the American National Election Studies first began measuring party identification in 1952" (p. 12). They also indicated that "During the 1970s and 1980s ... about a quarter of voters split their tickets–voting for presidential and congressional candidates for different parties. In recent elections, only about one voter in ten has cast a split-ticket ballot" (2018, p. 120). This polarization can also be seen in presidential approval ratings. In 2019, the Gallup polling organization reported that President Trump's approval during 2019 was 7% among Democrats and 89% among Republicans—the largest gap in the history of polling (Jones, 2020). It is clear that the American electorate has become increasingly polarized in recent years (see Klein, 2020).

The increasing ideological polarization has implications for trust in the news media. Between 1997 and 2016, trust in media dropped from 53% to 32% overall. However, distrust of the news media was sharply skewed to the ideological right; in 2016 only 14% of Republicans reported that they had trust in the media (Swift, 2016; we return to this contrast in chapter 8). The Knight Foundation

(2018) displays the contrasts in perceived media accuracy by ideology, highlighted in Figure 2.1.

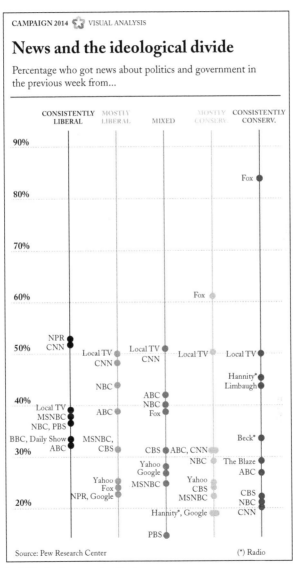

Figure 2.1. Perceived Media Accuracy by Ideology

Mitchell, A., Gottfried, J., Kiley, J., & Matsa, K. E. (2014, October 21). Media sources: Distinct favorites emerge on the left and right. PewResearchCenter. Accessed 11/10/16: http://www.journalism.org/2014/10/21/section-1-media-sources-distinct-favorites-emerge-on-the-left-and-right/

Ideological Placement of Each Source's Audience

Average ideological placement on a 10-point scale of ideological consistency of those who got news from each source in the past week...

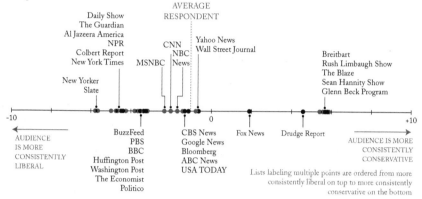

American Trends Panel (wave 1). Survey conducted March 19-April 29, 2014. Q22. Based on all web respondents. Ideological consistency based on a scale of 10 political values questions (see About the Survey for more details.) ThinkProgress, DailyKos, Mother Jones, and The Ed Schultz Show are not included in this graphic because audience sample sizes are too small to analyze.

PEW RESEARCH CENTER

Figure 2.2. Liberal and Conservative Content Sources

Mitchell, A., Gottfried, J., Kiley, J., & Matsa, K. E. (2014, October 21). Media sources: Distinct favorites emerge on the left and right. PewResearchCenter. Accessed 11/10/16: http://www.journalism. org/2014/10/21/section-1-media-sources-distinct-favorites-emerge-on-the-left-and-right/

It is interesting that Democrats rate Fox News at -87 while Republicans rate CNN at exactly the same level, -87.

Not surprisingly, different levels of trust in content sources results in different media diets. Mitchell, Gottfried, Kiley, and Matsa (2014) report that "nearly half (47%) of those who are consistently conservative name Fox News as their main source for government and political news." Although liberals display a greater diversity in media use than conservatives, patterns still emerge: "Among consistent liberals, CNN (15%), NPR (13%), MSNBC (12%) and the *New York Times* (10%) all rank near the top of the list." Liberals and conservatives tend to consume different content sources. Figure 2.2 displays this contrast visually.

One can see evidence of the balkanization of news media in a recent, extraordinary attempt to circumvent audience fragmentation. Foritin and Bronwich (2018) explained that "Sinclair Broadcast Group, the country's largest broadcaster … owns or operates 193 television stations …. Anchors on local stations owned by Sinclair Broadcast Group were forced to read identical scripts warning about 'fake news.'" The script in question declared that "'Unfortunately, some members of the media use their platforms to push their own personal bias and agenda to control exactly what people think,' dozens of news anchors said last month, reading from a script provided by Sinclair Broadcast Group." A fascinating video from *Deadspin* stitches together video from many anchors reading the required script (https://www.youtube.com/watch?v=aGIYU2Xznb4). Requiring almost 200 anchors to read the same script during the news is a clear attempt to reach viewers who consume balkanized media.

So, different groups of voters attend to different constellations of content sources. At this point we have explained how mass audiences have become fragmented. Some content overlaps between different content sources but much is different. When voters rely on different sources of information (e.g. opposing candidates who stress different groups of issues, different news media with contrasting content, or social media accounts with different information), their attitudes and behavior are inevitably influenced in different ways.

Figure 2.3 is designed to visually display the story we offer about media balkanization. On the left, we depict the network audience in the 1960s. The three major broadcast networks—ABC, CBS, and NBC—dominated the television scene, with a comparatively smaller audience watching PBS. The right side depicts the current state of media balkanization. ABC, CBS, NBC, and PBS continue to attract audiences, albeit smaller ones. Many new content sources have risen and

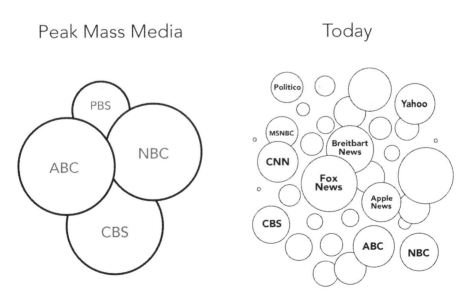

Figure 2.3. Shifts in Audiences and Content over Time

captured segments of the available audience. We note three reservations about this depiction. This figure is meant to show the three major broadcast network audiences as roughly equal; we did not attempt to correlate the size of any of these circles to specific market share (Table 2.1 displays difference in the audience for six networks). Second, the number and complexity of information sources today makes it impractical to display all of the overlap among these circles. Nor is it necessary to display all overlap make our basic point. Finally, newspapers (and other sources, such as *Time* or *Newsweek*) are omitted from this simplified model, but could be used in a similar model relating to print news balkanization with the same principles largely in place. We also want to observe that a variety of new content sources has emerged recently—particularly social media, but also such television networks as FOX News, CNN, and MSNBC. Figure 2.3 generally depicts the fall of mass media and the balkanization of content sources available to audiences.

More information is available today than ever before in history, in large part because of the potential of the Internet. Marr (2018), for instance, reported that 2.5 quintillion bites of data are created every day; over 90% of the data humans have generated were created in the last two years. We have an almost infinite array of information available to us today; but only the information (in messages) we attend and process can possibly influence our beliefs, values, and attitudes (Fishbein & Ajzen, 2010). So, if two groups of people attend to different news media, their beliefs and values will vary. We begin this argument by arguing that that "rhetoric is epistemic," that the messages we consume create and constitute what we consider to be knowledge.

Rhetoric Is Epistemic

The idea that rhetoric or communication is epistemic is a long-held and widely accepted notion (see, e.g. Baird, 1962; Bitzer, 1978; Farrell, 1990; Foss & Gill, 1987; Scott, 1967, 1976; Railsback, 1983; Weimer, 1977, 1981; see also the concept of the social construction of reality: Berger & Luckmann, 1966). The notion that rhetoric (or communication) is epistemic means that messages we consume create and shape knowledge, our conception of reality. "Knowledge" includes various cognitions, including beliefs or opinions concerning the nature, function, or value of objects and ideas as well as preferred courses of action.

The epistemic power of rhetoric or communication is not unlimited, for it cannot contravene what might be called "natural law" (although it could lead people to believe things that contravene "natural law"). For example, messages cannot make objects fall up—but it is possible, in certain circumstances, that a message could make some people believe things can fall up. Kenneth Burke's (1965) concept of the recalcitrance of reality is useful here. If there is rectangular object with a flat surface and four legs in front of you, we might be able to persuade you that it is a table or a desk. However, we almost certainly cannot make you think it is a duck or a truck, a comet or a locket. The media content consumed by voters (and non-voters) has important implications. Few people meet and interact with public figures (politicians, musicians, actors, corporate leaders, athletes) in person. Almost everything we know is learned through mediated messages. The content of these messages creates our beliefs, values, and attitudes.

Content of Messages Varies by Source

This claim may seem obvious but, because it is fundamental to our analysis, we provide support for this assertion here. First, candidates from different political parties emphasize different groups of issues in their campaign messages. Petrocik (1996) articulated Issue Ownership Theory, which focuses on political problems (issues), arguing that a political candidate should enjoy an advantage when voters believe that or she is better able to handle a problem than an opposing candidate. A party is said to "own" an issue when more voters think it can best address an issue than the opposing party. Perceptions that one party owns an issue develop in two ways. First, as time passes, political parties can acquire ownership of a particular issue:

> Party constituency ownership of an issue is much more long-term (although it can change and occasionally exhibits fluctuation) because its foundation is (1) the relatively stable, but different social bases, that distinguish party constituencies in modern party systems and (2) the link between political conflict and social structure. (p. 827)

Second, the "record of the incumbent creates a handling advantage when one party can be blamed for current difficulties" (p. 827). Such difficulties as "wars, failed international or domestic policies, unemployment and inflation, or official corruption" can provide the out party with a "'lease'–short-term ownership–of a performance issue" (p. 827). Owning or leasing an issue has the same potential advantage in elections.

Petrocik notes that "the campaigns waged by the candidates increase the salience of some problems, and, in doing so, cause voters to use their party linkage perception of the issue handling ability of the candidates to choose between (or among) them" (p. 827). The basic idea here is that when a candidate emphasizes an issue during an election campaign that stress should have an agenda-setting effect (see, e.g. McCombs, 2014; McCombs & Shaw, 1972; Weaver, McCombs, & Shaw, 2004), increasing the salience of that issue for voters. Presumably, issues of higher salience (more important to a given voter) will exert a greater influence on their voting behavior. For example, an ABC/*Washington Post* poll form

2018 asked which political party would do a better job handling various problems (see Table 2.2). Not surprisingly, voters were split on every issue. Nevertheless, if you were a Democrat, you would surely prefer that most voters thought such Democratically-owned issues such as health care and global warning were important. Conversely, Republicans would likely want most voters to think the economy and border security were important. If a candidate's issues become more important to voters that should benefit them at the polls.

Table 2.2. Which Political Party Would Do a Better Job Handling this Issue?

	Democratic	Republican
Health Care	50%	34%
Global Warming	50%	34%
Economy	39%	48%
Border Security	39%	49%

ABC News/*Washington Post* survey from 10/29-11/1/18 (PollingReport.com, 2019).

Several studies offer evidence to support Issue Ownership Theory. Petrocik (1996) provided public opinion polls from 1988–1991 on a number of issues to indicate which parties owned those issues at that point in time.

> Democrats are seen as better able to handle welfare problems. Perceptions of the parties on moral issues (e.g. crime and protecting moral values) favor the GOP. The data also document the GOP's hold on foreign policy and defense through the late 1980s. Opinions were mixed on economic matters, but were generally a GOP asset (by an average of about 13 points). Government spending, inflation, and taxation were also Republican issues. (p. 831)

The data confirmed the existence of issue ownership patterns among voters during this time period.

Petrocik (1996) investigated the question of whether candidates tend to use campaigns to stress issues owned by their own political party. Content analysis of *New York Times* coverage of the presidential campaign from 1952–1988 revealed that "presidential candidates emphasize issues owned by their party, although there are notable election and party differences" (p. 833). Petrocik, Benoit, and Hansen (2003–2004), employing data from 1952–2000, found that both nomination acceptance addresses and general television spots confirm issue ownership predictions (although they noted a tendency for presidential candidates to emphasize Republican issues more than Democratic issues overall, arguing that Republicans tend to own more national issues than Democrats). Data on election debates and television spots from the Functional Theory of Political Campaign Discourse (see Benoit, 2014a, 2014b) also confirm that Democrats stress Democratic issues more than Republicans, whereas Republicans emphasize Republican issues more than Democratic issues.

Enter the era in which both parties claim Issue Ownership via labels that are spun in various manners. Famous word influence consultant Frank Luntz (2007) has made a career of doing so, showing how a side can own a previously unowned issue through simple wordsmithing. For instance, while Democrats can own environmental issues, Republicans lay claim to oil drilling by labeling it "energy exploration." Meanwhile, both sides can lay claim to being on the "right" side of whether taxes should accrue after one passes away with one side (Democrats) arguing for using "estate tax" while another side (Republicans) claiming the unfairness of the same premise by calling it a "death tax." Democrats are likely to talk about "freedom of choice" whereas Republicans discuss the "right to life." Messages from different sources have distinctive content at many levels.

Other studies have investigated the effects of issue ownership on voters. Ansolabehere and Iyengar (1994) found that messages on Democratic issues were more effective when they were attributed to Democratic than Republican sources (and messages on GOP issues were more persuasive when the sources was thought to be a Republican rather than a Democrat). Simon (2002) found that candidates were less persuasive when they engaged in "dialogue" on the other party's issues. Abbe, Goodliffe, Herrnson, and Patterson (2003) report that when a candidate and a voter agree on what is the most important issue facing the electorate, the voter is more likely to vote for that candidate if that issue is owned by the candidate's political party. Finally, Petrocik, Benoit, and Hansen (2003/2004; see also Petrocik, 1996) report that there is a strong relationship "between the vote and the issue ownership bias of the problems of concern to the electorate" (p. 617). Theory and research on Issue Ownership confirm that different news sources (in this case, candidate messages and news coverage of candidates) stress different groups of issues. This differential emphasis influences voter behavior. So, political candidates (and parties) stress different sets of issues—or offer different content.

Differences in content occur between news media as well as between candidate messages. The Pew Research Center (2017) found that in 2012 MSNBC stressed commentary and opinion more than factual reporting (85% to 15%). FOX had slightly more commentary/opinion than factual reporting (55% to 45%) whereas CNN emphasized factual reporting somewhat more than commentary/opinion (54% to 46%). So, different media offer different content to consumers. Similarly, Smart (2019) counted the number of times various topics appeared in chyrons (text displayed at the bottom of the screen) on CNN, MSNBC, and FOX from August 2017 through January 2018. The investigation into Russia, operationalized through seven terms, was covered most by MSNBC. Hillary Clinton, measured with use of six words, was discussed most by FOX. The NFL protest (players such as Colin Kaepernick kneeling during the national anthem) was also covered more often by FOX than CNN or MSNBC.

A relatively recent phenomenon enabled by the Internet is the practice of second or "dual-screening." This activity occurs when a person watches television—the first screen—while simultaneously accessing a second screen such as a laptop, a smartphone, or tablet (see, e.g. Brown-Devlin, Devlin, Billings, & Brown, 2020). Typically, the television is the first screen and another device is the second screen. Of course, one may look at another device (such as a smartphone) while using a laptop. Many people are dual-screen users, which makes this an important phenomenon to understand. For example, Kirkpatrick (2017) reported that "an estimated 177.7 million U.S. adults—70.3% of the total population—will regularly use another digital device while watching TV this year." We want to note two implications of the use of dual screens. First, any second screen that attracts your attention—shifting it, at least in part, away from the first screen—will reduce comprehension and potentially degrade the gratifications obtained from that first screen. Second, the second screen often provides additional information to the user, information that reinforces or rejects the content consumed on the first screen, say watching a basketball game while commenting about it with friends using a smartphone (see Cunningham & Eastin, 2017). Such concepts are a prong of dual-screen usage dubbed "Social TV" (Kramer, Winter, Benninghoff, & Gallus, 2015). To the extent that some viewers dual screen while others do not, this practice further balkanizes consumption of the media. Moreover, if two dual screeners do use different content on their second screen, that further balkanizes media consumption. For instance, two people watching a series finale of *Homeland* could both be participating in dual-screen usage, yet one might be using the second screen to discuss key plot points on Twitter (enhancing the primary screen experience) while the other might be using the second screen to answer emails while casually "keeping track of" the episode (detracting from the primary screen experience). Not only would these viewings be demonstrably different but also one would be seen as hyper-engagement with *Homeland*, while the other would be seen as moving toward ambivalence toward *Homeland*.

Indeed, each source covers issues on continuums that vary widely. Where one once tuned in for "news," at the turn of the century, this content fragmented into elements such as "liberal news" or "conservative news." Now there are balkanized brands well beyond that. One can contrast liberal/conservative reporting vs. discussion/outrage and well beyond. Managing literacy within such an environment is daunting even for the ardently interested media literate consumer. Enter companies like Ad Fontes media, with continually-updated graphs used to help guide the reader on two core benchmarks: overall source reliability and political bias. Here, for instance, was how the companies' late 2019 model was advanced:

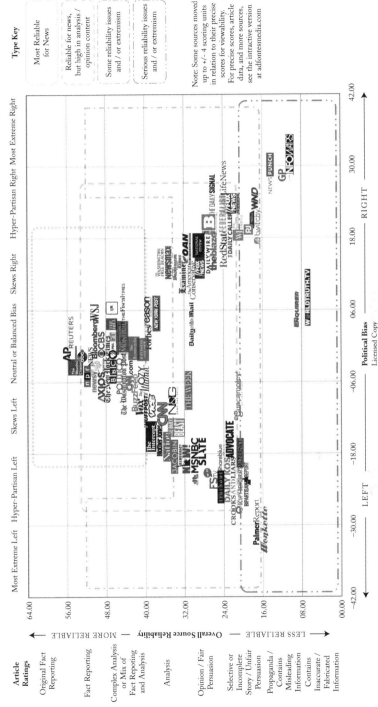

Figure 2.4: Ad Fontes Media Bias Chart (Ad Fontes Media, 2019)

Of course, this is a rabbit hole that is easy to go down and difficult to find one's way back. From most accounts, Ad Fontes is doing its level best to relay accurate placement of news courses, yet clearly one could debate each decision. Hence, there are likely going to be partisan outlets creating their own charts that place either liberal or conservative leaning outlets at the height of reliability and the center of bias metrics. Those sources will then place a high reliability bias centrist outlet like the Associated Press at one end of the spectrum, and realities on source vetting will inevitably diverge.

The fragmentation of news largely evolves from the form of decision tree one sees depicted in the Ad Fontes graphic. For a conservative, a small shift to the right moves one from, say, ABC News to the still very reliable *Wall Street Journal*. However, that *Wall Street Journal* shift moves one a bit closer to Fox News, generally acknowledged as a less reliable and more partisan source. The Fox News shift moves one ever closer to something truly abhorrent in information dissemination, such as *InfoWars*. Meanwhile, the same systematic siphoning can occur on the left: ABC News begets *Axios*, which begets *Mother Jones*, which begets the also abhorrent *Palmer Report*. The feeling that people from different places in the political spectrum cannot talk to each other anymore happens gradually within that process to the point that agreed-upon facts can no longer constitute the core of a substantive discussion.

Politics is by nature controversial. Reasonable people can disagree about many issues. On such issues, some questions simply do not have a "correct" or "incorrect" answer. People may *believe* that abortion should be prohibited by law or that everyone in America should be provided with health care but even really strong beliefs in controversial areas are not true or false. Some elements of the issue may be "facts" (empirically verifiable) but many ideas (particularly values) are not. However, when ideologically divergent content sources address the same issue, their content seemingly *must* be in conflict. The difference, largely, is in the default assigned. Whereas mass news used to default to neutral valence and then diverge when warranted, balkanized news defaults to divergence, only merging back to neutral when one side of an issue is dubbed truly unpalatable.

We can see that different groups of people attend to or consume different constellations of information sources (such as news media, Facebook, Twitter). Can it come as a shock that many conservatives tend to use conservative content sources while liberals are prone to consume liberal content sources? Different information sources offer different information and people cannot be influenced by information they did not consume; however, it is possible that they will be influenced by their particular media diet. Because messages are epistemic, people who consume messages with different content are likely to have different perceptions of the world and different attitudes toward people and policies. Content sources from one side of the political spectrum may vilify sources and reduce the credibility of opposing voices on controversial issues.

How Information from Messages Is Processed

Next, we explain how people can process the information in the messages they consume. Prior (2007) explained that three elements influence:

> the acquisition of political knowledge: opportunity, motivation, and ability (Delli Carpini & Keeter, 1996; Luskin, 1990). Opportunity refers to the availability of political information; ability, to people's skills in absorbing and comprehending the available information; and motivation, to whether people are actually interested in doing so. (p. 28)

Media balkanization has influenced opportunity to acquire information, U&G addresses motivation to select information sources, and ability is related to information processing (ability is also related to presence of distractions and other factors). Voters do not simply accept the information they acquire; not only do they consume different constellations of content sources with different information, but they process that information differently and produce different attitudes.

Lodge and Taber (2013) present theory and research on how voters process the information in various messages. People possess "partisan goals, which motivate them to apply their reasoning powers in defense of a prior, specific conclusion" (p. 150; see also Kruglanski & Webster, 1996). These partisan goals are embodied in their thoughts. Fishbein and Azjen (2010) argue that beliefs (loosely speaking, "facts,") and values (preferences) comprise the building blocks of attitudes. Some writers discuss cognitions and feelings or affect as related concepts. Lodge and Taber (1996) argue for the "hot cognition" thesis: "Affect is primary in our theory because it arises first in the stream of processing, is unintentional, and is difficult to control" (p. 20). "When an individual is exposed to a communication, the concepts in the message—whether consciously attended to or not —begin to activate the attendant concepts in *long-term memory*. Once a concept is activated, its activation spreads to all of its related concepts" (1996; see also Collins & Loftus, 1975). So, exposure to a message triggers affects (feelings) which color subsequent processing of arguments and evidence in messages. Again, existing attitudes influence how we process the messages we consume.

The upshot of hot processing is that we are inclined to interpret and evaluate a new message in line without existing attitudes. The "spreading effect" means that when an idea or person (e.g. immigration, Hillary Clinton) in a message is identified by the media consumer, other concepts (our beliefs, values, and attitudes) connected to that stimulus in long-term memory are activated. For example, when some Republicans hear the name "Obama" or see an image of Barack Obama, this stimulus could immediately activate or bring to mind such concepts as African-American, Obamacare, born in Kenya, or assault weapons ban. These concepts are likely to have negative affect toward Obama (be associated with unfavorable values) for many conservatives. This trigger could evoke some of the same ideas in Democrats (probably not "born in Kenya"), but in that case with positive affect. A Republican confronted with the name "Trump," or an image of Donald Trump could have ideas such as these triggered: businessman, Trump Tower, "The Apprentice," or real estate mogul. Some similar ideas might be activated in Democrats, with the possible addition other ideas such as married three times or repeated bankruptcies. So, as soon as a person identifies the topic of a message—before he or she begins processing the ideas, arguments, and evidence of a message—recognition of the topic of that message activates cognitions in long-term memory that influence subsequent message processing. We want to note that we are not claiming that all Republicans have negative feelings toward African-Americans. Nor do we claim that all Democrats have negative feelings about *The Apprentice*. We argue that some members of these groups of message consumers are likely to have different sets of cognitions and affect—and different reactions to a message.

The activation of related cognitions can be triggered by images (say, of a candidate or a gun), or by words (such as "Mitch McConnell," "Nancy Pelosi," "gun control," or "immigrant"), or by sounds (such as upbeat or ominous music/sound effects). Before we can begin considering the arguments and evidence in the message, our feelings, ideas, emotions related to that initial trigger are activated and influence our subsequent thoughts. Research has shown that voters view their preferred candidate more favorably than they view the opposing candidate. Jarman (2005), for example, examined reactions to the second general election presidential debate in 2004. Those viewers reacted more favorably to comments from the candidate of their own party than to comments by candidates of the opposing party. In other words, people interpret a given message differently depending on their attitudes.

After the initial stimulus from a message primes our affect, we begin thinking about a message's ideas (arguments and evidence) and biased processing can occur. Is the processing of information and arguments always biased? No, biases do not always color our thinking. However, Lodge and Taber (2000, pp. 184–185) explain that bias in cognitive processing of is most likely to occur when:

> one's attitudes are challenged (Kunda, 1990; Stevens & Fiske, 1995)
> an affective judgment is called for (Fazio, 1995)
> one's attitude is strong (Abelson, 1987; Krosnick & Petty, 1995)
> the consequences of being wrong are weak (Tetlock, 1985)
> the judgmental task is complex (Eagly & Chaiken, 1993)
> "objective" evidence is not readily available or the evidence is ambiguous
>   (Tversky & Kahneman, 1974)
> disconfirming evidence is not highlighted (Klayman & Ha, 1987)
> counterarguments come easily to mind (Lord, Ross, & Lepper, 1979)
> one is distracted or under time pressure (Petty & Cacioppo, 1986).

Some of the circumstances identified here occur commonly in political messages: for example, challenge to attitudes, affective judgments, strong attitudes, counterarguments come easily to mind (see our discussion of fake news and coordinated political defenses below).

Taber, Cann, and Kucsova (2009) conclude that there is "strong and consistent evidence of an *attitude congruence bias*, a *disconfirmation bias*, and a resultant *attitude polarization*" (p. 153; emphasis original; see also Kraft, Lodge, & Taber, 2015; Lord, Ross, & Lepper, 1979; Taber & Lodge, 2006). A congruence bias means that arguments which support a person's prior attitudes are perceived to be more powerful than arguments for the other side. So, for example, liberals have a tendency to see arguments for gun control as stronger than arguments opposing gun control. In the same way conservatives are prone to think that arguments against gun control are more powerful than arguments against such policies.

On the other hand, a disconfirmation bias means that people have a tendency to counter-argue evidence for the other side (see Petty & Cacioppo's [1981, 1986] Elaboration Likelihood Model); existing attitudes can actually be strengthened in the face of contradictory evidence. When exposed to arguments that contravene their own attitudes people often discount, diminish, or reject those arguments. For instance, if a person who opposes legalizing marijuana for recreational use encounters a pro-legalization messages, that person may think about their conviction that pot is a gateway drug. Kraft, Lodge, and Taber report "The results of many empirical studies" show that partisans "systematically denigrate, deprecate, and counterargue evidence that is contrary to their political views but accept uncritically the supportive evidence" (2015, pp. 121–122). Not surprisingly, research found that people recalled more positive than negative information about the preferred candidate as well as more negative than positive information about the opponent (Meffert, Chung, Joiner, Waks, & Garst, 2006). This analysis of the primacy of affect and the subsequent processing of message content does not mean conversion (attitude change) is impossible. It does mean that reinforcement of existing attitudes is more likely to occur given the way humans process stimuli and how they store and access information.

The hostile media effect (HME; Vallone, Ross, & Lepper, 1985) argues that people are inclined to perceive news stories as biased against their own ideological interests and in favor of opposing ideological interests. Meta-analysis has confirmed the existence of this phenomenon (Hansen & Kim, 2011). The HME plays a role in the disconfirmation bias, inclining us to reject messages that disagree with our existing attitudes. If we accidentally attend to a news story that disagrees with our existing attitudes, we are likely to reject that story (we discuss charges of "fake news" below).

Meanwhile, third-person effect (TPE; Davison, 1983) becomes conflated within our news reception process. Typically, TPE is applied to persuasive stimulus, say an advertisement or political speech. The theory postulates that individuals will often presume such persuasion to have more effect on others than on themselves, which, of course, is conceptually impossible. Similar to Garrison Keillor's conception of a Lake Wobegon in which "all the children are above average," TPE aids in explaining how audiences can be persuaded even when they insist a stimulus has no effect. However, the concept of *news* as a persuasive stimuli is a relatively new concept in which individuals must grasp. Prior generations (the ones living in the age of Walter Cronkite as discussed in our previous chapter) often viewed news more objective, unlike the persuasive ads offered in commercial breaks. Information was the core content; persuasion was what paid the bills to allow the objective information to be advanced. Of course, now that is much more blurred, leading to individuals who think they can objectively watch a news program all while acknowledging its biases or placement on the Ad Fontes chart. Third-person effect would tell us, yet again, that such attitude change happens much more rarely than individuals would think.

Incessant Attacks on "Fake News"

We argue that the disconfirmation bias, and the hostile media effect, have been heightened in contemporary political discourse by a systematic attempt to vilify groups of information sources, reducing their credibility and hence their persuasiveness. Criticism of the "liberal media" was expressed over half a century ago.

During his presidential run, the media bedeviled Republican Barry Goldwater. His press secretary even handed out gold pins to reporters that read "Eastern Liberal Press"; some blamed the media for Goldwater's loss to Democrat Lyndon Johnson in the 1964 presidential campaign (Hemmer, 2014). Four years later, after Richard Nixon ran against Hubert Humphrey, an analysis of news coverage of the Nixon-Humphrey presidential campaign published in *The News Twisters* claimed a bias toward Humphrey and against Nixon. As a result,

> Nixon ordered Special Counsel Charles Colson to get the book on the *New York Times* bestsellers list. Colson ferreted out which stores' sales were used to determine the list, and bought up every copy they had. And it worked: Efron's book became an official *New York Times* bestseller. (For years, Nixon staffers stumbled upon boxes crammed full of *The News Twisters*.) (Hemmer, 2014)

Vice President Spiro Agnew advanced an alliterative attack on critics of Nixon, calling them the "nattering nabobs of negativism" (Agnew, 1970). The Vice President lamented the "narrow and distorted picture of America [that] often emerges from the televised news" (1969). It came out that President Nixon had an "enemies list." On June 27, 1973, the Senate Watergate Committee released two lists of enemies: a top twenty list (referred to as the original list) and another list of 207 people or organization, about 60 of whom worked in the media. These lists included several syndicated columnists (Jack Anderson, Saul Friedman, Joseph Kraft, Max Lerner, Mary McGrory, and Gary Wills), Ed Guthman (*LA Times*), William Eaton (*Chicago Daily News*), James Doyle (*Washington Star*), William Hines (*Chicago Sun Times*), Martin Nolan (*Boston Globe*), Thomas O'Neill (*Baltimore Sun*), John Pierson (*Wall Street Journal*), Robert Manning (*Atlantic*), Paul Samuelson (*Newsweek*), James Reston (*New York Times*), Stanley Karnow (*Washington Post*). James Laird (*Philadelphia Inquirer*), John Osborne (*New Republic*), Ted Knap (*New York Daily News*), Richard Rovere (*New Yorker*), Clayton Fritchey (*Harpers*), Robert Sherrill (*Nation*), several television correspondents (Marvin Kalb and Daniel Schorr, CBS; along with Sander Vanocur NBC), and several newspapers (*The New York Times, Washington Post, St. Louis Post Dispatch*). A second, longer list of enemies was released later (Axtell, 2017; Benac, 2017). The President obviously disliked the media, although his distrust was a secret until these disclosures.

Later criticism of media were public. Rush Limbaugh (2017) explained that "I have spent all of these years attempting to get people to know what they're watching and know what they're reading when they consume media and how to spot the bias, the unfairness, the bigotry, all of the things that the media is. It has been a never-ending quest." These ideas laid the ground work for Donald Trump's attacks on "fake news" and charges that the news media are the "enemy of the people."

The attack on the veracity of news media, particularly liberal media, arguably is rooted in the critiques made by talk show host Rush Limbaugh. *The Rush Limbaugh Show* was nationally syndicated in 1988. He claims to reach 14 million people every day and 27 million listeners every week. "He is a critic of liberalism in the US and liberal bias in the widespread media" ("Rush Limbaugh," 2020). We do not argue that Limbaugh was the first to rail against the liberal media, but he is a particularly loud and consistent voice on this topic.

President Trump has repeatedly attacked the news media for reporting "fake news." For example, in a press conference held in February of 2017, about a month after he took office, the President offered several assertions about the news:

Russia ... was all fake news .... It's all fake news. It's all fake news.

Russia is fake news, Russia—this is fake news put out by the media.

The news is fake because so much of the news is fake.

The reporting is fake.

Very fake news now.

Reince [Priebus] is working so hard just putting out fires that are fake fires. They're fake. They're not true.

But I want to just tell you, the false reporting by the media, by you people—the false, horrible, fake reporting makes it much harder to make a deal with Russia.

The President repeatedly advanced the claim that the media present "fake news." Stelter (2018) reported that "between January 20, 2017 [Trump's inauguration] and today [1/17/18] Trump has used the word 'fake' at least 404 times in tweets and public appearances." Many other Republicans echo his attacks—and his defenses—in what seems to be a coordinated effort to vilify news media that reports stories unfavorable to the GOP. Research has shown that repetition of ideas (such as "fake news" or "witch hunt") can reinforce beliefs and values (attitudes; see, e.g. McCullough & Ostrom, 1974).

President Trump took this line of attack on news media even further, declaring the fake news to be "the enemy of the people":

On February 17, 2017, President of the United States Donald Trump declared on Twitter that *The New York Times*, NBC News, ABC, CBS, and CNN were "fake news" and the "enemy of the people." Trump repeated the assertion on February 24 at the Conservative Political Action Conference, saying, "A few days ago I called the fake news the enemy of the people and they are. They are the enemy of the people." At a June 25, 2018 rally in South Carolina, Trump singled out journalists as "fake newsers" and again called them "the enemy of the people." ("Enemy of the People," 2019)

So, if a conservative voter accidentally happens upon a message from a liberal news outlet, that voter may very well reject the information from that source as false. Of course, Democratic voters could also reject information form conservative sources, but the Republicans generally, and President Trump specifically, have consistently harped on the claim of fake news, so it seems likely that conservatives will dismiss news as fake more often than liberals.

Recently the Trump campaign created a web page (www.snowflakevictory) informing supporters "How to win an argument with your liberal relatives." This page has links to 12 arguments for use against relatives with conflicting ideology ("snowflake" is a derogatory term that has been applied to liberals):

The Trump Economy is Strong

It is important to enforce immigration law & Build the Wall

Other countries are finally paying their fair share

Trump is improving our trade deals

Trump approach to health care much better than Dems, who would kill employer-provided healthcare.

Trump is expanding his reach to beyond just his base—women, Latinos & Black support is growing.

Trump tax cuts fueled the economy, Dems would raise taxes on everybody by repealing the Trump tax cuts.

There was no quid pro quo, Democrats are always obsessed with impeachment.

Joe Biden threatened to withhold $1 billion in aid from Ukraine unless they fired the prosecutor looking into the company where his son worked. That has NOT been debunked.

BIG GOVERNMENT SOCIALISM

Trump is proving it's possible to have a strong economy and a clean environment at the same time.

The U.S. is again a world leader in energy production, but Democrats would eliminate all fossil

fuel production under the Green New Deal (which means 10 million jobs lost and higher heating and cooling bill

This webpage encouraged Trump supporters to argue with relatives who do not support the current president—over Christmas! It provided ammunition for this fight in the form of praise of Trump, defenses of the president, and attacks on the opposition (the irregular use of capitalization and periods after each link, as well as a left parenthesis without a corresponding right parenthesis, are original).

This analysis could be seen as hostile to Republicans generally and President Trump in particular. This is not our intent. Other politicians have criticized the news media. For example, Vice President Spiro Agnew complained about the liberal news media. He charged that they were elite, privileged, and "intellectually dishonest" (Holden, 2019). Democrats have also criticized the news media (Easley, 2019). Nevertheless, no previous U.S. president has attacked the news media as systematically and vehemently as President Trump. Chris Wallace argued that President Trump has "engaged in the most direct sustained assault on freedom of the press in our history" (Cole, 2019). We believe that no previous American president has had such consistent support from ideologically-based content sources (including Fox News). Furthermore, evidence provided earlier showed that Republicans had less than half as much trust in the news as Democrats (Swift, 2016). Similarly, Sutton (2017) reported that "Fifty-five percent of Republican respondents believed that fake news was reported on intentionally by traditional news outlets to advance a specific agenda, compared to 41 percent of independents and 24 percent of Democrats." Not only do most attacks on "fake news" come from the right, this claim is accepted by more Republicans than Democrats. The need for traditional forms of journalism is more critical now than ever before.

In fact, President Trump has attempted to alter the public record to suit himself. On the first of September, 2019 President Trump tweeted that Alabama, Florida, South Carolina, North Carolina, and Georgia would "most likely be hit harder than anticipated" by Hurricane Dorian (Law & Martinez, 2019). The Birmingham National Weather Service station almost immediately tweeted that "Alabama will NOT see any impacts from #Dorian." "We repeat, no impacts from Hurricane #Dorian will be felt across Alabama" (Law & Martinez, 2019). Then, the President ordered an aide to pressure the National Oceanic and Atmospheric Administration, which oversees the National Weather Service, to change its stance to be consistent with Trump (Baker, Friedman, & Flavelle, 2019). The NOAA issued a statement disavowing the Birmingham weather station's tweet (this incident was the one in which the President displayed a map of the area showing Dorian's projected path, with included a crude alteration of the path, apparently with a Sharpie, to include Alabama). So, President Trump actually ordered the public record altered to be consistent with his tweet. Attacks on the media come from both sides of the ideological spectrum, but are made most often from the right.

Conclusion

The first chapter chronicles the rise of mass communication. This chapter has argued that the mass media has become balkanized, that content sources have proliferated and new outlets often offer niche content. Because rhetoric is epistemic, the information we consume in messages creates our perception of reality, our beliefs, values, and attitudes. The way in which human beings process information (the primacy of affect, congruence bias, and disconfirmation bias means that our perception and evaluation of messages is likely to be influenced by our cognitions. In the case of President Trump, the frequent refrain of "fake news" and advancement of an apparently coordinated defense of the Republican president may provide a justification and an incentive to reject information that conflicts with the beliefs of many conservatives.

References

Abbe, O. G., Goodliffe, J., Herrnson, P. A., & Patterson, K. D. (2003). Agenda setting in congressional elections: The impact of issues and campaigns on voting behavior. *Political Research Quarterly, 56*, 419–430.

Abelson, R. (1987). Conviction. *American Psychologist, 43*, 267–275.

Abramowitz, A. I. (2018). *The great alignment: Race, party transformation, and the rise of Donald Trump*. New Haven: Yale University Press.

Abramowitz, A. I., & Webster, S. W. (2015). The rise of negative partisanship and the nationalism of U.S. elections in the 21st century. *Electoral Studies, 41*, 12–22.

Abramowitz, A. I., & Webster, S. W. (2018). Negative partisanship: Why Americans dislike parties but behave like rabid partisans. *Advances in Political Psychology, 39*, 119–135.

Ad Fontes Media (2019). Media Bias Chart 4.1. Retrieved on November 15, 2019 at: https://www.adfontesmedia.com/?v=402f03a963ba

Agnew, S. (1969, November 13). Television news coverage. Accessed 7/14/16: http://www.americanrhetoric.com/speeches/spiroagnewtvnewscoverage.htm.

Agnew, S. (1970, September 11). Address by the Vice President, California Republican State Convention. University of Maryland Library.

Ansolabehere, S., & Iyengar, S. (1994). Riding the wave and claiming ownership over issues: The joint effects of advertising and news coverage in campaigns. *Public Opinion Quarterly, 58*, 335–357.

Arceneaux, K., & Johnson, M. (2013). *Changing minds of changing channels? Partisan news in an age of choice*. Chicago: University of Chicago Press.

Axtell, D. G. (2017). The complete Nixon's enemies list. Accessed 7/27/17: http://www.enemieslist.info/list1.php.

Baird, A. C. (1962). Speech and the "New" philosophies. *Central States Speech Journal, 13*, 241–246.

Baker, P., Friedman, L., & Flavelle, C. (2019, September 11). Trump pressed top aide to have Weather Service "clarify" forecast that contradicted Trump. Accessed 12/5/19: https://www.nytimes.com/2019/09/11/us/politics/trump-alabama-noaa.html.

Baldasty, G. J. (1992). *The commercialization of news in the nineteenth century*. Madison, WI: University of Wisconsin Press.

Balkanization. (2019). *Wikipedia*. Retrieved at: https://en.wikipedia.org/wiki/Balkanization.

Beevolve. (2017). An exhaustive study of Twitter users across the world. Retrieved at: http://www.beevolve.com/twitter-statistics.

Benac, N. (2017, February 17). Remember Nixon: There's History behind Trump's Attacks on the Press, Associated Press, February 17, 2017. This statement was first reported by the *Washington Post*'s Bob Woodward and Carl Bernstein.

Bennett, B., & Wilson, C. (2019, December 16). The way we fight back. *Time*, pp. 48–54.

Benoit, W. L. (2014a). *A functional analysis of political television advertisements* (2nd ed.). Lanham, MD: Lexington Books.

Benoit, W. L. (2014b). *Political election debates: Informing voters about policy and character.* Lanham, MD: Lexington Books.

Benoit, W. L., & Glantz, M. (2017). *Persuasive attack on Donald Trump in the 2016 Republican primaries.* Lanham, MD: Lexington Books.

Benoit, W. L., & Holbert, R. L. (2010). Political communication. In C. R. Berger, M. E. Roloff, & D. R. Roskos-Ewoldsen (Eds.), *Handbook of communication science* (2nd ed., pp. 437–452). Thousand Oaks, CA: Sage.

Berger, P. L., & Luckmann, T. (1966). *The social construction of reality*. London: Penguin Books.

Bitzer, L. F. (1978). Rhetoric and public knowledge. In D. Burks (Ed.), *Rhetoric, philosophy, and literature* (pp. 67–93). West Lafayette: Purdue University Press.

Brown-Devlin, N., Devlin, M. D., Billings, A. C., & Brown, K. A. (2020). Five rings, five screens?: A global examination of social TV influence on social presence and social identification during the 2018 Winter Olympic Games. *Communication & Sport*. Accessible via Online First, last accessed on March 24, 2020 at: https://journals.sagepub.com/doi/10.1177/2167479519899142

Burke, K. (1965). *Permanence and change*. Indianapolis: Bobbs-Merrill.

Cable television in the United States. (2020). *Wikipedia*. Accessed 2/4/20: https://en.wikipedia.org/wiki/Cable_television_in_the_United_States.

Cambridge Dictionary (2018). Mass communication. Accessed 12/22/18: http://dictionary.cambridge.org/us/dictionary/english/mass-communication".

Campbell, K. K., & Jamieson, K. H. (1978). *Form and genre: Shaping rhetorical action*. Falls Church, VA: Speech Communication Association.

Cole, B. (2019, December 13). Trump is behind "most direct sustained assault" on media freedom says Fox News Host Chris Wallace. Accessed 1/1/20: https://www.newsweek.com/donald-trump-chris-wallace-fox-news-media-freedom-assault-1477093.

Collins, A., & Loftus, E. (1975). A spreading-activation theory of semantic processing. *Psychological Review, 82*, 240–247.

Commission on Presidential Debates (2019). Debate history. Accessed 11/26/19: https://www.debates.org/debate-history/1960-debates/.

Cunningham, N. R., & Eastin, M. S. (2017). Second screen and sports: A structural investigation into team identification and efficacy. *Communication & Sport, 5,* 288–310.

Davison, W. (1983). The third-person effect in communication. *Public Opinion Quarterly, 47*(1), 1–15.

Demographic History of the United States: Historical Census Population. (2019). *Wikipedia.* Accessed 7/9/19: https://en.wikipedia.org/wiki/Demographic_history_of_the_United_States.

Dimmick, J. W. (2010). *Media competition and coexistence.* London: Routledge.

Eagly, A., & Chaiken, S. (1993). *The psychology of attitudes.* Fort Worth, TX: Harcourt Brace Jovanovich.

Easley, J. (2019, August 14). Democratic contenders unload on news media. *The Hill.* Accessed 12/28/19: https://thehill.com/homenews/campaign/457302-democratic-contenders-unload-on-news-media.

Enemy of the People. (2019). *Wikipedia.* Accessed 11/29/19: https://en.wikipedia.org/wiki/Enemy_of_the_people#United_States.

Farhi, P. (2020, January 22). First day of Senate impeachment trial becomes a modest TV hit with 7.5 million watching during prime time. *Washington Post.* Accessed 2/4/20: https://www.washingtonpost.com/lifestyle/style/first-day-of-senate-impeachment-trial-becomes-a-modest-tv-hit-with-75-million-watching-during-prime-time/2020/01/22/1d8ff2d2-3d41-11ea-8872-5df698785a4e_story.html.

Farrell, T. B. (1990). From the Parthenon to the bassinet: Death and rebirth along the epistemic trail. *Quarterly Journal of Speech, 76,* 78–84.

Fazio, R. (1995). Attitudes as objective-evaluation associations: Determinants, consequences, and correlations of attitude accessibility. In R. Petty & J. Krosnick (Eds.), *Attitude strength: Antecedents and consequences* (pp. 247–282). Hillsdale, NJ: Lawrence Erlbaum Associates.

Fishbein, M., & Ajzen, I. (2010). *Predicting and changing behavior: The reasoned action approach.* New York: Psychology Press.

Foritin, J., & Bronwich, J. E. (2018, April 2). Sinclair made dozens of local news anchors recite the same script. *New York Times.* Accessed 12/17/19: https://www.nytimes.com/2018/04/02/business/media/sinclair-news-anchors-script.html.

Foss, S. K., & Gill, A. (1987). Michel Foucault's theory of rhetoric as epistemic. *Western Journal of Speech Communication, 51,* 384–401.

Gill, K. (2016, March 23). What is the Fairness Doctrine? About.com. Accessed 12/3/16: http://uspolitics.about.com/od/electionissues/a/fcc_fairness_2.htm.

Gunther, M. (1999, June 15). The transformation of network news. *Nieman Reports.* Accessed 11/11/16: http://niemanreports.org/articles/the-transformation-of-network-news/.

Hansen, G. J., & Kim, J. (2011). Is the media biased against me? A meta-analysis of the hostile media effect research. *Communication Research Reports, 28,* 169–179.

Hemmer, N. (2014, January 17). The conservative war on liberal media has a long history: Roger Ailes's success at Fox News is unique, but the project of creating a right-leaning alternative to established media stretches back to the 1940s. *The Atlantic.* Accessed 2/18/18:

https://www.theatlantic.com/politics/archive/2014/01/the-conservative-war-on-liberal-media-has-a-long-history/283149/.

History of Radio. (2018). *Wikipedia* Accessed 12/22/18: https://en.wikipedia.org/wiki/History_of_radio.

Hobsbawn, E. (1994). *The age of extremes: A history of the world, 1914–1991.* New York: Pantheon Books.

Holden, C. (2019, November 10). Fifty years ago—Spiro Agnew and the "Des Moines" speech. Accessed 12/8/19: https://www.desmoinesregister.com/story/opinion/columnists/2019/11/10/fifty-years-ago-spiro-agnew-and-des-moines-speech/4166207002/.

Jamieson, K. H., & Capella, J. N. (2008). *Rush Limbaugh and the conservative media establishment: Echo chamber.* Oxford: Oxford University Press.

Jarman, J. W. (2005). Political affiliation and presidential debates: A real-time analysis of the effect of the arguments used in the presidential debates. *American Behavioral Scientist, 49,* 229–242.

Jones, J. M. (2020, January 21). Trump third year sets new standard for party polarization. *Gallup.* Accessed 2/4/20: https://news.gallup.com/poll/283910/trump-third-year-sets-new-standard-party-polarization.aspx.

Katz, E., Blumler, J. F., & Gurevitch, M. (1973). Uses and gratifications research. *Public Opinion Quarterly, 37,* 509–523.

Kirkpatrick, D. (2017). EMarketer: 70% of US adults "second-screen" while watching TV. *MarketingDive.* Accessed 1/5/20: https://www.marketingdive.com/news/emarketer-70-of-us-adults-second-screen-while-watching-tv/510341/v.

Klayman, J., & Ha, Y. W. (1987). Confirmation, disconfirmation, and information in hypothesis testing. *Psychological Review, 94,* 211–228.

Klein, E. (2020). *Why we're polarized.* New York: Avid Reader Press.

Knapton, S. (2016, January 20). Facebook users have 155 friends. *Telegraph.* Accessed 2/17/17: http://www.telegraph.co.uk/news/science/science-news/12108412/Facebook-users-have-155-friends-but-would-trust-just-four-in-a-crisis.html.

Knight Foundation. (2018). Perceived accuracy and bias in the news media. *Gallup.* Accessed 7/4/10: https://kf-site-production.s3.amazonaws.com/publications/pdfs/000/000/255/original/KnightFoundation_AccuracyandBias_Report_FINAL.pdf.

Knobloch-Westerwick, S. (2015). *Choice and preference in media use: Advances in selective exposure theory and research.* New York: Routledge.

Kraft, P. W., Lodge, M., & Taber, C. S. (2015). Why people "don't trust the evidence": Motivated reasoning and scientific beliefs. *Annals of the American Society of Political and Social Science, 658,* 121–133.

Kramer, N. C., Winter, S., Benninghoff, B., & Gallus, C. (2015). How 'social' is Social TV? The influence of social motives and expected outcomes on the usage of Social TV applications. *Computers in Human Behavior, 51,* 255–262.

Krosnick, J., & Petty, J. (1995). Attitude strength: An overview. In R. Petty & J. Krosnick (Eds.), *Attitude strength: Antecedents and consequences* (pp. 1–247). Hillsdale, NJ: Lawrence Erlbaum Associates.

Kruglanski, A., & Webster, D. (1996). Motivated closing of the mind: "Seizing" and "freezing." *Psychological Review, 103*, 263–283,

Kunda, Z. (1987). Motivation and inference: Self-serving generation and evaluation of evidence. *Journal of Personality and Social Psychology, 53*, 636–647.

Lang, A. (2000). The limited capacity model of mediated message processing. *Journal of Communication, 50*, 46–70.

Law, T., & Martinez, G. (2019, September 8). NOAA disputes its own experts, siding with President Trump over Hurricane Dorian and Alabama. Here's a full timeline of the controversy. Accessed 12/6/19: https://time.com/5671606/trump-hurricane-dorian-alabama/.

Leung, L. (2013). Generational differences in content generation in social media: The roles of gratifications sought and of narcissism. *Computers in Human Behavior, 29*, 997–1006.

Limbaugh, R. (2017, June 28). The Trump administration calls out the fake news. *Rusha Limbaugh.com.* Accessed 2/18/18: https://www.rushlimbaugh.com/daily/2017/06/28/donald-trump-is-destroying-the-drive-by-media/.

List of most-liked Facebook pages. (2019). *Wikipedia.* Accessed 6/2/19: https://en.wikipedia.org/wiki/List_of_most-liked_Facebook_pages.

List of most watched television broadcasts in the United States. (2019). *Wikipedia.* Accessed 7/9/19: https://en.wikipedia.org/wiki/List_of_most_watched_television_broadcasts_in_the_United_States.

Lodge, M., & Taber, C. S. (2000). Three steps toward a theory of motivated political reasoning. In A. Lupia, M. D. McCubbins, & S. L. Popkin (Eds.), *Elements of reasoning: Cognition, choice, and the bounds of rationality* (pp. 183–213). Cambridge: Cambridge University Press.

Lodge, M., & Taber, C. S. (2013). *The rationalizing voter.* Cambridge: Cambridge University Press.

Lord, C. G., Ross, L., & Lepper, M. R. (1979). Biased assimilation and attitude polarization: The effects of prior theories on subsequently considered evidence. *Journal of Personality and Social Psychology, 37*, 2098–2109.

Lowry, B. (1997, September 2). Cable stations gather strength. *LA Times.* Accessed 12/12/16: http://articles.latimes.com/1997/sep/02/entertainment/ca-28033.

Luntz, F. (2007). *Words that work: It's now what you say, it's what people hear.* New York: Hyperion.

Mark, M. (2019, November 15). The number of Americans watching Trump's impeachment hearings on TV pales in comparison to Nixon. Accessed 11/25/19: https://www.businessinsider.com/trump-impeachment-tv-viewership-comparisons-2019-11.

Marr, B. (2018, May 21). How much data do we create every day? *Forbes.* Accessed 11/27/19: https://www.forbes.com/sites/bernardmarr/2018/05/21/how-much-data-do-we-create-every-day-the-mind-blowing-stats-everyone-should-read/#6c34940e60ba.

Matthews, D. (2011, August 23). Everything you need to know about the Fairness Doctrine in one post. *Washington Post.* Accessed 2/24/18: https://www.washingtonpost.com/blogs/ezra-klein/post/everything-you-need-to-know-about-the-fairness-doctrine-in-one-post/2011/08/23/gIQAN8CXZJ_blog.html?utm_term=.179706e5206a.

McCombs, M. E. (2014). *Setting the agenda: Mass media and public opinion*, 2nd ed. Malden, MA: Polity Press.

McCombs, M. E., & Shaw, D. L. (1972). The agenda setting function of the mass media. *Public Opinion Quarterly, 36,* 176–187.

McCullough, J. L., & Ostrom, T. M. (1974). Repetition of highly similar messages and attitude change. *Journal of Applied Psychology, 59,* 395–397.

McGarr, M. E. (1986). *The decline of popular politics.* New York: Oxford University Press.

McQuail, D., Blumler, J. G., & Brown, J. (1972). The television audience: A revised perspective. In D. McQuail (Ed.), *Sociology of Mass Communication* (pp. 135–165). Middlesex, England: Penguin.

Meffert, M. F., Chung, S., Joiner, A. M., Waks, L., & Garst, J. (2006). The effects of negativity and motivated information processing during a political campaign. *Journal of Communication, 56,* 27–51.

Miller, G. A. (1956). The magic number seven plus or minus two: Some limits on our cognitive capacity to process information. *Psychological Review, 63,* 81–97.

Mitchell, A., Gottfried, J., Kiley, J., & Matsa, K. E. (2014, October 21). Media sources: Distinct favorites emerge on the left and right. PewResearchCenter. Accessed 11/10/16: http://www.journalism.org/2014/10/21/section-1-media-sources-distinct-favorites-emerge-on-the-left-and-right/.

Nielsen. (2016, March 17). Are Americans watching the Republican or Democratic debates—or both? Accessed 11/12/16: http://www.nielsen.com/us/en/insights/news/2016/are-americans-watching-the-republican-or-democratic-debates-or-both.html.

Noam, E. M. (2009). *Media ownership and concentration in America.* Oxford: University Press.

Petrocik, J. R. (1996). Issue ownership in presidential elections, with a 1980 case study. *American Journal of Political Science, 40,* 825–850.

Petrocik, J. R., Benoit, W. L., & Hansen, G. L. (2003–2004). Issue ownership and presidential campaigning, 1952–2000. *Political Science Quarterly, 118,* 599–626.

Petty, R. E., & Cacioppo, J. T. (1981). *Attitudes and persuasion: Classic and contemporary approaches.* Dubuque, IA: William C. Brown.

Petty, R. E., & Cacioppo, J. T. (1986). *Communication and persuasion: Central and peripheral routes to attitude change.* New York: Springer-Verlag.

Pew Research Center. (2006, March 13). Network evening news ratings. *Pew Research Center.* Accessed 1/4/19: http://www.journalism.org/numbers/network-evening-news-ratings/.

Pew Research Center. (2017, August 16). On MSNBC, opinion dominates reporting. Accessed 11/27/19: https://www.journalism.org/2013/03/17/the-changing-tv-news-landscape/1-on-msnbc-opinion-dominates-reporting/.

PollingReport.com. (2019). Democrats vs. Republicans. Accessed 11/27/19: https://www.pollingreport.com/dvsr.htm.

Printing Press. (2018). *Wikipedia.* Accessed 12/22/18: https://en.wikipedia.org/wiki/Printing_press.

Prior, M. (2007). *Post-broadcast democracy: How media choice increases inequality in political involvement and polarizes elections.* Cambridge: Cambridge University Press.

Quartz. (2018). Watch: The first TV commercial, which aired 75 years ago today. *Wikipedia.* Accessed 12/22/18: https://qz.com/721431/watch-the-first-tv-commercial-which-aired-75-years-ago-today/.

Railsback, C. C. (1983). Beyond rhetorical relativism: A structural-material model of truth and objective reality. *Quarterly Journal of Speech, 69,* 351–363.

Rush Limbaugh. (2020). *Wikipedia.* Accessed 1/1/20: https://en.wikipedia.org/wiki/Rush_Limbaugh.

Sabato, L. J., Kondik, K., & Skelley, G. (2016, November 17). 16 for '16: Bite-sized observations on a wild election. *Sabato's Crystal Ball: University of Virginia Center for Politics.* Accessed 12/14/19: http://crystalball.centerforpolitics.org/crystalball/articles/16-for-16/.

Satellite Television in the United States. (2020). *Wikipedia.* Accessed 2/4/20: https://en.wikipedia.org/wiki/Satellite_television_in_the_United_States.

Schneider, M. (2019, December 26). Most-watched television networks: Ranking 20019's winners and losers. *Variety.* Accessed 2/4/20: https://variety.com/2019/tv/news/network-ratings-top-channels-fox-news-espn-cnn-cbs-nbc-abc-1203440870/.

Scott, R. L. (1967). On viewing rhetoric as epistemic. *Central States Speech Journal, 18,* 9–17.

Scott, R. L. (1976). On viewing rhetoric as epistemic: Ten years later. *Central States Speech Journal, 27,* 258–266.

Simon, A. F. (2002). *The winning message: Candidate behavior, campaign discourse, and democracy.* Cambridge: Cambridge University Press.

Smart, C. (2019). The difference in how CNN, MSNBC, & Fox cover the news. *The pudding.* Accessed 11/27/19: https://pudding.cool/2018/01/chyrons/.

Statista. (2016). Leading ad supported broadcast and cable networks in the United States in 2015, by average number of viewers. Accessed 11/11/16: https://www.statista.com/statistics/530119/tv-networks-viewers-usa/see bmp C:\b\RiseFall MassComm\tv-networks-viewers-usa-.

Statista. (2019). Leading social networks in the U.S., 2018. Accessed 6/2/19: https://www.statista.com/statistics/247597/global-traffic-to-leading-us-social-networking-sites/.

Statista. (2019). Twitter: Number of monthly active U.S. users 2010–2019, Accessed 6/6/19: https://www.statista.com/statistics/274564/monthly-active-twitter-users-in-the-united-states/.

Stelter, B. (2015, August 7). Fox's GOP debate had record 24 million viewers. *CNN.* Accessed 6/15/16: http://money.cnn.com/2015/08/07/media/gop-debate-fox-news-ratings/.

Stelter, B. (2018, January 17). Trump averages a "fake" insult every day. Really. We counted. *CNN Business.* Accessed 12/6/19: https://money.cnn.com/2018/01/17/media/president-trump-fake-news-count/index.html.

Stevens, L., & Fiske, S. (1995). Motivation and cognition in social life: A social survival guide. *Social Cognition, 13,* 189–214.

Sutton, K. (2017, March 29). Poll: 6 in 10 Americans think traditional news outlets report fake news. *Politico.* Accessed 3/29/17: http://www.politico.com/story/2017/03/fake-news-monmouth-poll-media-236639.

Swift, A. (2016, September 14). Americans' trust in mass media sinks to new low. *Gallup.com*. Accessed 11/21/16: http://www.gallup.com/poll/195542/americans-trust-mass-media-sinks-new-low.aspx.

Taber, C. S., Cann, D., & Kucsova, S. (2009). The motivated processing of political arguments. *Political Behavior, 31* 137–155.

Taber, C. S., & Lodge, M. (2006). Motivated skepticism in the evaluation of political beliefs. *American Journal of Political Science, 50*, 755–769.

Tetlock, P. E. (1985). Accountability: A social check on the fundamental attribution error. *Social Psychology Quarterly, 48*, 227–238.

Tolentino, J. (2019). *Trick mirror: Reflections on self delusion*. New York: Random House.

Trump, D. (2017, February 16). Remarks by President Trump in Press Conference. Accessed 2/10/17: https://www.whitehouse.gov/the-press-office/2017/02/16/remarks-president-trump-press-conference.

Tucker, D. R. (2017, July 31). How the repeal of the Fairness Doctrine gave us Donald Trump. *Washington Monthly*. Accessed 1/4/19: https://washingtonmonthly.com/2017/07/31/how-the-repeal-of-the-fairness-doctrine-gave-us-donald-trump/.

U.S. Census Bureau. (2019). U.S. and world population clock. Accessed 3/27/20: https://www.census.gov/popclock/.

Vallone, R. P., Ross, L., & Lepper, M. R. (1985). The hostile media phenomenon: Biased perception and perceptions of media bias in coverage of the "Beirut massacre." *Journal of Personality and Social Psychology, 49*, 577–585.

Weaver, D., McCombs, M., & Shaw, D. L. (2004). Agenda-setting research: Issues, attributes, and influences. In L. L. Kaid (Ed.), *Handbook of political campaign research* (pp. 257–282). Mahwah, NJ: Erlbaum.

Weimer, W. B. (1977). Science as a rhetorical transaction: Toward a non-justificational conception of rhetoric. *Philosophy & Rhetoric, 10*, 1–29.

Weimer, W. B. (1981). Why all knowing is rhetorical. *Journal of the American Forensic Association, 20*, 63–71.

Williams, B. A., & Delli Carpini, M. X. (2011). *After broadcast news: Media regimes, democracy, and the new media environment*. Cambridge: University Press.

World Population. (2019, June 1). *Wikipedia*. Accessed 6/1/19: https://en.wikipedia.org/wiki/World_population.

CHAPTER THREE

Not 'Must See' for Me: The Balkanization of Entertainment

In 1988, a genre-changing sitcom debuted to terrific ratings, instantly becoming the #2-rated comedy in all of television by garnering 38 million viewers per week. Named after its comedienne lead actress, *Roseanne* became a staple in the ABC comedy lineup, eclipsed in viewership only by NBC's *The Cosby Show*. After completing a successful nine-season run, the show returned 30 years after its debut with similar ranked-metric success: *Roseanne* was again the #2-rated comedy show in all of television (this time surpassed only by CBS stalwart *The Big Bang Theory*) and was, once again, a cornerstone of ABC programming. The only difference: *Roseanne* now only had 14 million viewers; even when adding time shifted DVR and streaming totals, the number only reached 17.8 million viewers, less than half the viewership of Season 1 in 1988 (de Moraes & Hipes, 2018).

Of course, the *Roseanne* story quickly took a political turn as the actress offered what most dubbed a racist tweet (Koblin, 2018), leading to her firing and the retooling of the program into a new show without her, *The Conners*. However, the parallel case is useful for understanding the rise and fall of communal television. The same program with the same overall ranking could do so with less than half the viewers from three decades prior. The media touchstones people could previously count on for common languages, popular culture references, and shared understanding largely have splintered (see Webster & Ksiazek, 2012). The last chapter referenced nonfiction-based media splintering, resulting in a cacophony of opinions and perspectives rarely in concert with one another. In the de-massified nonfiction world, we lose common facts and agendas. In the de-massified fiction/ entertainment world, we lose shared experiences and languages. This sounds less serious than when discussion politics, social issues, and world views, yet these same forms of scripted entertainment fragmentation results in less common conversations and, arguably, the loss of the popular. *Roseanne* is a great example of an ongoing change in thousands of other manners.

And it's not just television.

Consider, for a moment, music—more specifically, Billboard's standard competition for "Song of the Summer" (see full lists at Billboard Staff, 2018). Past winners are so ubiquitous in people's minds that they become the soundtrack in which memories unfold (can any teenager of the period not have either nostalgically sigh or disgustingly groan to every word of Bryan Adams' 1991 Song of the Summer, *Everything I Do (I Do It For You)*?). These songs are so well-known that they are still played in sports stadiums decades later (e.g. 1982 winner *Eye of the Tiger* [Survivor]), spark dance crazes (e.g. 1996 winner *Macarena* [Los Del Rio]) or create instant star longevity for the artist (e.g. 1999 winner, *Genie in a Bottle* [Christina Aguilera]). Compare that to modern winner of the Song of the Summer and the comparisons, generally, pale. Drake won the 2018 iteration of the competition with a song, *In My Feelings*, that sparked an online dance craze yet never led a single week of radio airplay. One-hit wonders have always been a staple of the list, yet it is clear that if you asked even younger demographics to sing along to a Song of the Summer by a one-hit wonder, they are far more likely to succeed with the 1992 winner, Sir Mix-A-Lot's *Baby Got Back,* than Omi's 2015 winner, *Cheerleader*. All of these are not to argue that a song from the past is *better* than another as much as to say recent winners are received *differently*—and by a dwindling overall share of the American audience.

At this point, some could be claiming such comparisons are merely a lament of times gone by; relics of opinions that the "good ol' days" were demonstrably better. However, this chapter will set out to make a case that is less to do with comparisons that are based on better/worse dichotomies and much more on notions of how dramatic shifts in media content offerings offer customization at the expense of widespread familiarity. This chapter will utilize many different types of media to make a two-pronged case: never have people have better matches between what they desire to consume and what is available for consumption AND never has the general public had less commonality in what they consume in virtually all forms of entertainment media. It is great to receive targeted, specified media content designed to optimize your experience. But there's a danger therein: we start to expect it—and reject anything that doesn't meet those narrow taste parameters.

More Competition = Less Hits?

One could reasonably conclude that this chapter, then, is arguing a line similar to Chris Anderson's (2006) *The Long Tail*, where hits are lessened and the tails of each part of the bell curve become increasingly important, but that presumption would be wrong. Societies need hits, nay they *demand* them. Even if the largest media product at a given time is not as large a swath as before, we still have metrics to apply to the standards of popular culture: A is greater than B, C, or D and is, hence, a *hit*. Every weekend still has a box office champion; Billboard does not fail to list a #1 song on the Hot 100 if it fails to be the hummable wallpaper to our lives that many hits have been in the past. We need hits because we need touchstones, but the manner in which we go about determining those touchstones is more varied than ever before. In many ways, entertainment media in the Year 2020 drowns out so much of the niche markets that whatever is left consumes all the oxygen of a medium. With so little oxygen in the room, only the rare signal within the noise (see Silver, 2012) can survive. That creates a long-lasting hit or seminal artist that perhaps is not as central as modern metrics would assume.

Consider popular music. As of November 2018, artists of the 21st Century Rihanna, Drake, Usher, and Beyonce all had more collective weeks at #1 on the Billboard Hot 100 than Michael Jackson or Elton John. However, all metrics are not created equal. Michael Jackson has sold 750 million albums and Elton John 300 million, whereas Usher has sold 65 million and Rihanna 60 million, less than 10% of Jackson's total. Drake set a new record in 2018 with a collective 29 weeks at #1 with three different hit songs, yet sold just sold 236,000 copies of the album those hits came from, *Scorpion*, in the first week out. The next week, *Scorpion* led again, yet with 29,000 total sales, a 27-year low for a weekly #1 album total (Resnikoff, 2018). Yes, metrics are different in modern times where streams (of which Drake had over two billion in 2018) override album sales. Yet, those streams are inherently more liquid and ephemeral than the permanent purchase of the album. The imprint of *Scorpion* (total sales: 4.5 million) will not be the equivalent of Michael Jackson's greatest album, *Thriller* (total sales: 66 million) even if the number of weeks at #1 would dictate Drake's dominance.

The point is that a #1 song today inevitably has lower mass audience penetration than before, meaning that those collective sing-alongs in sports stadiums and wedding ceremonies may be harder to accomplish with recent hits. If one were to consult chart records, one would assume the inverse should be true. On the country music chart alone, Florida Georgia Line's "Cruise" set a new record in 2013 with nearly a half year (24 weeks) at #1. This was then eclipsed in 2017 with Sam Hunt's "Body Like a Back Road" (34 weeks), before Florida Georgia

Line reclaimed the title by joining Bebe Rexha for "Meant to Be", a song with an incredible 50-week run at the top spot. Why have the three longest-running songs of all-time come in the last decade? Because everything else is niche—customized and specialized—to the point that very little is left at the center of that bell curve of popularity. To paraphrase Norma Desmond in *Sunset Boulevard*, the hits are still big, but it's the competition that got smaller.

This is not to say the hits of today match audience numbers with the hits of the past, though. When adjusting for inflation, just two of the top 20 highest box office grosses are from this century and neither of which (*Star Wars: The Force Awakens*, *Avatar*) are in the top 10. So what's going on here? How can we be living in an era in which songs and music artists are breaking all-time records and yet films are not even close? The answer can be found in the metrics that are used. Songs compete with each other *within a given time period*. People aren't listening to Drake in a higher proportion than they listened to Elvis, the Beatles, or Michael Jackson in their respective eras; however, Drake is one of the few hit artists that can singularly move the needle because he's largely competing with niches and customization. Films (via box office grosses) are competing *across time periods*. When doing so, one realizes that *Black Panther* was big, but not as big as *Titanic*. One also realizes that each industry has different "tentpoles", defined as films that have built-in audiences and, hence, built-in profits.

The degree to which a medium is built on tentpoles is largely determined by whether distribution outlets are finite or unlimited. Thus, films are limited to the roughly 40,000 screens available in theaters across America. It is not uncommon for a 14-screen multiplex to have four or five screens dedicated to the opening weekend of a tentpole film. This causes several results: the opening weekend take now regularly exceeds 60% of an overall run (making a film largely critic/Rotten Tomatoes-proof), films experience shorter theatrical runs (because another tentpole film demands the screens for its opening weekend), and films then move to video/streaming distribution more quickly than ever. Films also, then, have "hammocks", prestige projects that may or may not make money but are supported by multiple "tentpoles" that ensure profitability.

Music, of course, works entirely differently. There is no limit to the number of songs or albums one could access on iTunes, nor is there a maximum bandwidth to streaming a video on YouTube. The result becomes entirely different as well: songs gradually are discovered by different people over a multitude of weeks (lengthening the run), often are then bolstered by videos that are not released until many weeks into a run, and naturally have more repeat customers. After all, if you like a film, you may watch it a second time in the theater, but if you like a song, it may get hundreds of repeat listens on your personal music devices.

Other mediums work differently, too. Books largely follow the same paths as music (more options than ever on places like Amazon), people are not reading books more than ever, but the record-setters are mostly 21st Century entries such as the *Harry Potter* series and the author with the most entries on the *New York Times* Best Seller list is a modern one: James Patterson. We again want the viral hit (for a book club or merely a common conversation), yet those hits are manipulated and false in some demonstrable ways. In 2015, for example, politician Ted Cruz's biography, *A Time for Truth: Reigniting the Promise of America*, was excluded from the *New York Times* Best Seller list because of what was deemed "strategic bulk purchases" designed to make the book seem more popular than it was (Byers, 2015, para. 1). Indeed, the difference between purchasing and consuming a media product is difficult to decipher. Stephen Hawking's *A Brief History of Time*, for instance, is a book frequently bought and yet rarely read from beginning to end (Hawkins, 2018); it's a prestige book one displays to show intellect, yet not one likely to be discussed at a book club lest many of the readers be discovered as fake-readers of the tome.

Which brings us back to Drake: a respected pop artist who is, nevertheless, a perfect modern musical case of the popular arguably masquerading as uber-popular. In an attempt to keep up with modern metrics of music consumption, Billboard unveiled a new formula for determining the rankings on its Hot 100 chart. The formula became the equivalent of:

1 download = 75 streams = 1,000 airplays

This was slightly modified in 2018 to amplify paid streams over free ones (Hogan, 2018), yet the release of Drake's 25-track album, *Scorpion*, was so powerful in the model that every song (along with six others) made the Hot 100 in a single week. You read that correctly: Drake had 31 songs in the Hot 100 in a single week, one more than Michael Jackson had in his entire career (it would have been two more had a remastered song "Don't Matter to Me" [a collaboration of Drake with Jackson] not been on the list of Drake's 31 charting songs). At this point, one could simply want to say congratulations to Drake, but one must delve more deeply into what this accomplishment means. The majority of the charting songs were not released or receiving any airplays; in fact, we don't know the degree to which even the album purchasing fans listened to the album from beginning to end. Should a song be labeled a Hot 100 hit without any evidence that anyone had even listened to it?

If we still need hits (for cultural relevance and societal touchstones), it would seemingly behoove the process to be able to identify which ones are not just *purchased* but also *consumed*.

Films have fairly good metrics in this regard (one rarely purchases a ticket to a movie and fails to attend), yet music and books have more wobbly models, which not only makes the mass/hit/center less valid, but also makes one question whether such a center exists at all. One could also notice that television has not been mentioned at all in this part of the conversation—and that is because the metrics of measuring hit television have moved from one pole to another, as the medium moved from commercial broadcast networks to premium subscriptions to streaming dominance. Integrated within that is a principle we'll call the "HBO Model".

The HBO Model

In 1999, two prestige programs were introduced to the public, embraced by critics and viewers alike. Led by two visionary showrunners, Aaron Sorkin and David Chase, *The West Wing* and *The Sopranos* respectively became appointment television for many American—and later global—viewers. In many ways, their popularity and runs were similar: *The West Wing* garnered 95 Primetime Emmy Award nominations and 26 wins, *The Sopranos* had 111 Primetime Emmy nominations and 21 wins; both were highly popular and profitable on each network; *Wing* ended in 2006 after seven successful seasons, *Sopranos* ended in 2007 after six successful seasons.

Still, in other manners, the programs were quite different. *The West Wing* was on NBC, a commercial broadcast television network. This meant a wider audience reach, more episodes (22) expected for each season, a clearly delineated September-May release calendar, and roughly 42-minute episodes with appropriate pause breaks for commercials. Meanwhile, *The Sopranos* was on HBO, a premium broadcast network. This meant a more defined reach of dedicated subscribers who each paid roughly $10/month for all HBO content. Moreover, *The Sopranos* could vary in release date, episode length, and number of episodes, each of which HBO would program repeatedly on many different dates and time slots over the course of the week. The funding (and ultimate profitability) of each program was demonstrably different because of the networks that featured them. One could watch *The West Wing* without any subscription cost and without any connection to whether one found the rest of NBC's programming worth consuming. However, if one wanted to watch *The Sopranos*, one must dole out the subscription fee ($120/year). Whether someone watched only this program or, instead, sought out HBO programming each and every night made little difference to HBO's bottom line. With premium cable, you were either on the hook for $10/month or you were on the outside looking in for access to *The Sopranos* and many other zeitgeisty programs at the time, such as comedy *Sex and the City*.

Prior to the mainstreaming of HBO and, later, other subscription based programming, the models for determining the economic viability of entertainment were relatively easy to discern. The profit for a film was essentially:

Box Office Gross—Production Costs—Marketing/Promotion Costs = Profit/ Loss (+/-)

Music was a similar formula:

Album Sales—Production Costs—Marketing/Promotion Costs (often including tours as a loss leader) = Profit/Loss (+/-)

Even television was fairly easy to calculate, with the only real exception being that the rating (which largely determined advertising rates) could fluctuate substantially depending on four key factors: programming night, programming time slot, counterprogramming within the time slot, and lead-in program (known in the industry as "inheritance" (Eastman & Ferguson, 2012). Such factors could cause a viable program to be terminated early and could make a top-10 hit out of a program that critics consistently panned (hence the high ratings of forgettable NBC sitcom "hammocks" such as *Union Square* and *The Single Guy* in the 1990s, benefitting from programming slots between juggernauts like *Friends*, *Seinfeld*, *Frasier*, and *ER*). Lead-in alone accounted for more than 50% of a television rating. Profit (and subsequent viability as a program) hinged on these formulas, coupled with whether enough episodes could be produced and sold to affiliates in syndication.

However, subscription based services quickly moved beyond movie channels. Since most were getting television programming from cable or satellite providers, subscription fees became an increasing part of the equation. ESPN, for instance, in 2017, costs a customer over $9.00 per month (Gaines, 2017), meaning that the average cable/satellite subscribers pay over $100 per year, dwarfing the money that ESPN could make from advertising. Other channels benefitted from such an arrangement, albeit to a lesser degree than ESPN. Debates ensued about paying for channels one wasn't watching (the irony that all subscribers simultaneously subsidize the salaries of liberal icon Rachel Maddow and Sean Hannity was not lost), yet, in the end, ala carte programming cost even more. If the History Channel cost the average subscriber a quarter per month yet only 10% of the people wanted that channel, the cost would increase 1,000% to $2.50 per month if purchased ala carte.

The result was the "great American cable-TV bundle" (Smith, 2018, para. 1)—and a prioritization of event/must-see programming over a balanced programming lineup. In essence, the HBO Model became *the* programming model for the majority of channels. For instance, American Movie Classics rebranded as AMC, producing just a few original programs but enough for people to insist they be included in the bundle; if one wanted their 13 episodes per year of *Mad Men*, *Breaking Bad*, one had to pay for all of AMC's programming. A single must-have program (such as AMC's later massive hit, *The Walking Dead*) meant a heightened subscriber fee for a network offering B-movie programming the large majority of the time. Sports channels were particularly adept at the "must have" item surrounded by less-watched programming; the SEC Network is watched in extremely small numbers the majority of the time, yet often as a key conference game on the channel—just enough to assure that it justifies its inclusion (and fee) with a demonstrable portion of cable and satellite subscribers. One would think this would create a sharks and minnows dichotomy (ratings winners surrounded by a vast majority of ratings underperformers). However, what happened was that the sheer number of channels (peaking at an average of 189 channels per household in 2014; Nielsen Insights, 2014) each had must-see programming, yet for niches—not masses—of fans. The average cable/satellite subscriber was only watching 17 of these channels (Nielsen Insights, 2014), but each was a uniquely different *combination* of must-have programming. Put simply, many were rushing home to watch the program they craved, but fewer people were craving the same offerings.

And then came Netflix.

Zero to 700 in Five Years Flat

When defining the overall sense of "Americana", one often refers to anything that a majority of Americans do. In 2016, two trends hit that tipping point—but going in opposite directions. The number homes with a telephone landline dropped below the 50% mark (Kastrenakes, 2017) while the number of households with Netflix subscriptions moved above the 50% mark (McAlone, 2017). Both were products of rapid wireless permeation. The seismic shift in Netflix subscribers went from one-third to one-half of America in just three short years, and it happened because of original programming. A company with HBO-like roots in feature film distribution and a monthly fee model, Netflix developed and released political pot-boiler *House of Cards* of February 1, 2013, followed several months later by *Orange is the New Black*, a pair of shows that would start a frenzy of original programming from media service providers not limited to Netflix (with upwards of 700 original shows by the end of 2018; Spangler, 2018) but expanding to Amazon, Hulu, CBS All Access, and many, many others.

These services still had the subscriber fees, yet deviated from the HBO Model in ground-shifting manners. First, the companies were entirely streaming entities; hence, there were no Nielsen ratings one could access. We know that HBO's

Sopranos averaged 10 million live viewers per week, but the entirety of Netflix's library? No one outside of the company truly has any numbers as the company's policy is not to release them. Much like radio in its migration from terrestrial (and Arbitron-monitored ratings) to Sirius/XM Satellite radio (with no ratings mechanism at all), the move to streaming also represented a move from the quantifiable to the unmeasurable. Some could argue that the entire point of Netflix is about narrowcasting, not about broadcasting and there is truth to that assessment if only examining the conundrum from the Netflix monetary perspective. As Heisler (2016) explains, "the bedrock of Netflix's original content strategy is to provide a selection of content that appeals to every type of viewing interest, no matter how niche" (para. 8). Nevertheless, when seeking to determine whether *Stranger Things* is a desirable watercooler program when compared to *Narcos*, one is quickly befuddled.

Second, Netflix, Amazon, Hulu, and others did not just change the amount and accessibility of original programming, it also altered the pace in which one consumed it. This was just an escalated version of what came before in the form of the DVD box set. For example, the television show *24* was novel in that of 24 annual episodes represented an hour of real-time in the storyline. It was released in traditional weekly installments, but many opted to skip the weekly airing on FOX in favor of the purchase/rental of a full season box set in which all episodes could be consumed in a long day or weekend.

Netflix programs then became the streaming equivalent of the season box set, releasing episodes a season at a time—and then later designing an interface that automatically began the next episode upon completion of the previous one, creating an opt-out—as opposed to an opt-in—form of binge-watching. In contrast, many of Hulu's programs were offered in weekly installments, yet the nature of the online subscription service still enhanced the desire to binge-watch; if there was only one program one wanted to consume on Hulu, it was financially advantageous to wait until a queue of new episodes had accumulated before subscribing rather than committing to the service on a continual basis.

The more people embraced these subscription services, the more binge-watching became en vogue, partly because people liked it, but also partly because people felt they had to consume episodes rapidly to avoid spoilers from others who had completed a binge. One could only talk about a program when they knew others were "caught up", reducing watercooler effects and emphasizing personalized habits over industry-dictated practices.

The end result is a model of media balkanization similar to what we offered in the last chapter, only now with entertainment options plugged into the splintering rather than news. Figure 3.1 uses scripted television programming as the exemplar for the differences we are advancing.

As the Figure shows, when people watched television programs in the 1980s, there were far fewer options (even the few cable TV options were often showing re-runs and going off-air in non-peak hours). Thus, not only did *Dallas* or *The Cosby Show* draw large audiences, but the same audiences were often familiar (and watching) both. Summers were deserts for launching any new programming, only cementing these shows in people's psyches by offering second-run and sometimes even third-runs of each program. All seven seasons of *The Golden Girls* were offered on Saturday nights, now considered a wasteland in which no broadcast network offers new programming at all, let alone expecting a massive hit like *The Golden Girls* was.

Turning to the right side of the model, note that it is just as cluttered—if not more so—than the left side. We still watch massive hours of scripted programming, but in so many different ways and tastes that rarely do the audiences meet. One's media diet can consist, quite entirely, of reality programs or crime dramas and yet never have the need to re-watch something because nothing else is available. Virtually all audiences are smaller than even the mid-range ratings of the 1980s programs, yet people find plenty of high-quality programming to watch. We can rightly claim an era of "Peak TV" all while not agreeing at all as to which programs constitute that pinnacle of scripted programming. The options are balkanized, fragmented, and customized. They also are rarely overlapping.

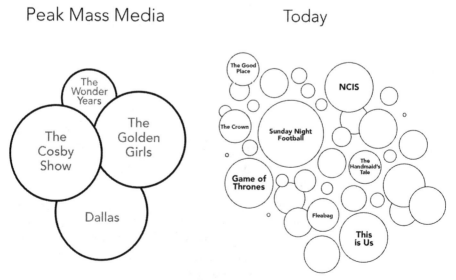

Figure 3.1. Entertainment Balkanization Model

Mediated Entertainment is Dead; Long Live Mediated Entertainment!

At this point, one could (perhaps rightly) argue that while the live/same time consumption numbers are a shadow of what they were for each media device/platform from decades prior, the key is that people still consume media-based entertainment more than ever ... just at different times and different paces and with different devices. And that's true. Television viewing remains high over-all—nearly six hours of consumption per day (Fisher, 2019); Screen time is at a stunning zenith: Americans now spend over 11 hours per day staring at screens (Fottrell, 2018); while work-related activities, gaming, and other aspects of modern life occupy some of this time, the majority is still spent consuming media.

The desire to listen to music has not dissipated.
The desire to watch feature-length movies has not dissipated.
The desire to watch episodic television has not dissipated.

Over thirty years after *America's Funniest Home Videos*, we are still just as likely to enjoy a short video with an unfortunate pratfall. Everything has changed and yet nothing has changed. The only way to explain such a paradox is through similar veins to what was outlined earlier in this chapter.

The first manner to explore these tastes and attitudes is via the advent of niche content. The amount of *consumption* has not changed. The amount of *content* available to consume most definitely has. When Anderson (2006) penned his book *The Long Tail*, he wrote of the 98% rule, where people presumed the tails of such long content distribution curves were empty, filled with books left unsold, songs left unplayed, videos left unwatched—and yet 98% of most content was being consumed at least once every three months. Anderson concluded that "where the economics of traditional retail ran out of steam, the economics of online retail kept on going" (p. 9).

Nearly 15 years later, the world Anderson described is now on steroids. YouTube, for instance, has 432,000 hours (49.3 years) of content uploaded *per day* (MerchDope, 2018). Arguably more telling is the average number of views per video: 5,676. Such a viewership means (a) there's an audience for the large majority of videos uploaded to the platform and (b) that audience is small enough to not be viable in any previous traditional media manner. When content creation and distribution nears the domain of free, niche content becomes the equivalent of personalizing one's media consumption world.

A second explanation for the paradox would be to argue these tastes are not about the type of content being consumed; it is all about the timing. The pace. Aristotelian *kairos*. People may enjoy the same type of programs, yet do so at a demonstrably different pace, so much so that defining what constitutes "binge-watching" remains elusive (Jenner, 2016). One could say three or more episodes in a single sitting, yet this could mean a mere hour (when eliminating commercials) of a favorite TV show would constitute binge-watching, while watching a dozen in one night with breaks in between might not. But that's just part of the story—the acceleration of content consumption. The other pertains to the timing in which the consumption occurs.

When all media becomes time-capsuled, the time in which you consume it can ascribe new meaning. The TV show *24* debuted just two months after the tragedy of September 11, 2001, featuring torture-based interrogation techniques that some justified as warranted in a post-9/11 era. When people consumed this program years later, they might now know more about waterboarding and the flaws in such intelligence gathering techniques because of the real-life events that followed. Contexts change. In 2018, Paramount television planned to debut a television version of the 1989 cult film, *Heathers*, featuring plotlines about mass shootings and other forms of school-based violence. The debut was timed for March, yet the aftermath of the mass shooting at Marjory Stoneman Douglas High School forced the program to be tabled (Petski, 2018b) until October 25. When it did, it was offered in binge-watched form (multiple episodes per night for five consecutive nights) and, even then, one night was not shown because of a mass shooting at a synagogue in Pittsburgh (Petski, 2018a). In having these real-life intrusions into the reception of the storyline, *Heathers* becomes an optimal example for explaining how the time and circumstance in which one consumed the program has the potential to alter how it is received.

Sports: The (Occasional) Exception

The 2017 National Football League season was wrought with controversy and concern for the continued dominance of the top media product in America. Anthem protests—including a sharp rebuke from President Trump, safety concerns, and a lack of competitiveness of teams from the largest media markets led to fears that the Super Bowl rating would still be dominant, but not what it once was. Even the quarterback from one of the participating teams, the Philadelphia Eagles' Nick Foles, was a journeyman backup elevated to the starting job because of an injury. And yet …

Super Bowl LII drew 103.4 million viewers in 2018 (Otterson, 2018), the tenth-highest rating in U.S. television history. Ratings were down from the previous Super Bowl game, but still not problematic. When taking into account the entirety of NFL seasonal ratings, games still constituted the highest-rated programming on five major networks: CBS, NBC, Fox, ESPN, and the NFL Network. The Super Bowl—and the league itself remained ensconced as the "symbolic cultural heart" (Burton, 2017, para. 48) of the nation, evidenced economically by the $7.8 billion in annual television contracts (Novy-Williams, 2017).

The opening example of this chapter told the story of ABC situation comedy *Roseanne*, achieving #2-rated comedy status in two different eras all while achieving a rating more than double its value in the former year (1988) than the latter (2018). Such trends then played out in a variety of contexts and platforms in the core of the chapter that unfolded. This downward trend is mass consumption naturally begs the question: is there any form of media that has been immune to the de-massification of mass media? That answer comes in the form of sports products, yet with an asterisk to be explained in a bit.

Consider this Super Bowl example. The 2018 domestic viewership of Super Bowl LII was 103.4 million; its 1988 counterpart was Super Bowl XXII, watched by 80.1 million viewers. The rating actually increased, largely doing so in similar proportion (29%) to the American population growth over those 30 years (31%). Lest you think this is merely a football story, consider that NBA regular season ratings are hitting new highs while the 2017 NBA Finals was the largest rating in two decades (Holloway, 2018). Similar stories could be told from established sports like golf to rising-interest sports like mixed-martial arts. Even if ratings are not rising for a given sports product, a flat rating such as the latest ones for the horse racing's Kentucky Derby can still be construed as a major ratings coup when all other programming genres are dropping substantially. As Anderson (2006) predicted, there are fewer "hits" than ever before, but what has rapidly become clear is that among those hits, sports represent the epicenter. At the time of this writing, over 80% of the highest ratings in television history are sport-related; over half of those have been achieved in the Internet era.

Of course, not all sports programming is immune, and the sports that did suffer ratings decline did so because of the same trends forming the crux of this book: niche media offerings, personalization, and fragmentation. For instance, national baseball and hockey ratings have experienced significant decline. As Traina (2018) notes, "unless it's the postseason, the days of baseball moving the needle nationally are over" (para. 2).

The culprit, most likely, is the regionalization of sports channels and packages. Growth of *Major League Baseball Extra Innings* or hockey's *NHL Center Ice* makes interest more local. For instance, if someone is a fan of the Kansas City Royals, they can watch each of 162 regular season games (roughly 500 hours) via Fox

Sports Kansas City or *Major League Baseball Extra Innings*. If games are on every night, a true Royals fan will always select the Royals game, leaving any national broadcast behind. *NFL Sunday Ticket* does not create a similar quandary because one's favorite teams play only 16 games (roughly 50 hours), leaving more time for fans of a team to consume other games that don't include their favorite/local market. The result? Football stays national and defies de-massification trends while everyday sports like baseball become regional—still with highly-loyal fan bases, but with that loyalty being to the team much more than to the league.

In the end, sports seem different than all other forms of media content precisely because they *are* different. The number of programs, YouTube clips, film offerings, and songs continues to grow as production and distribution costs near zero (we will discuss this in the context of Moore's Law in the next chapter; Moore, 1965) yet sports have approximately the same number of epic, must-see games. Every year, there is one Super Bowl, one Masters Golf tournament, one Daytona 500 race. There is not one song, one movie, or one TV show that matches with the pinnacle sports events (although a TV series' final episode comes closer than any other episode). Other offerings could conceivably compete with the traditional old-guard cornerstones of sport, yet largely do not as the desire for live, immediate, watercooler sports programming makes sports the last game in town.

Enter the FAANG Marketplace

All experts seemingly agree that the content consumption game has changed; they just can't agree on how many game changers are present and, if so, what the ramifications are. Galloway (2017) refers to "the four", labeling Amazon, Apple, Facebook, and Google (alphabetically) while jointly classifying them as "engaged in an epic race to become the operating system for our lives" (p. 9). Webb (2019) utilizes these four while expanding with more global aims, creating a "big nine" moniker consisting of Microsoft, Apple, IBM, Google, Amazon, Facebook, Tencent, Alibaba, and Baidu. She does so with a more ominous tone, noting that "the big nine corporations may be inadvertently building and enabling vast arrays of intelligent systems that don't share our motivations, desires, or hopes for the future of humanity".

However, when considering the technological giants most directing affecting media consumption tastes and habits, the acronym FAANG (Facebook, Apple, Amazon, Netflix, Google [Alphabet]) is arguably the most accurate form of lexicon. Representing just 1% of the S&P 500, these entities constitute half of the top-ten most valued stocks while possessing a collective net worth of three *trillion* dollars (Momoh, 2018). These five stocks collectively were ascribed tremendous power because they appeared "so resistant to price drop and to trend so steadily upward" (Navin, 2018, para. 1). It's not difficult to see why; Amazon, for instance, now possesses over 100 million subscribers to Amazon Prime, equating to over two-thirds of American households (Del Rey, 2018). That's remarkable audience penetration in the modern age. More Americans can access Amazon's *The Marvelous Mrs. Maisel* than most cable networks, including ESPN, CNN, and FOX News. Amazon does so through niche marketing—not just for its products, but for its ubiquitous content: from music to movies to television programs, Amazon has options. Even that holiest of grails, the National Football League, now has a streaming contract with Amazon. However, such penetration shows the limitations of de-massified media: if FAANG companies have largely penetrated the American market with disposable income and yet some technology giants are turning meager profits, one must inevitably question whether such a model is sustainable.

Netflix's success in securing an audience has already been established earlier in this chapter, with 137 million subscribers. Yet the company has done so while still maintaining over $8 billion of debt (Spangler, 2018), leading one to wonder how much people will be willing to pay in the future to maintain quality, personalized, content-free programming.

Such ubiquity has tremendous potential, yet is not without limitations. By creating customized programming for the consumer, FAANG companies offer bliss for the at-home consumer, yet do so with operating costs that are difficult to justify the expense. By the end of 2018, all five stocks were officially classified as being in "bear markets" (Kelleher, 2018, para. 1), with some of the key cylinders of the new media economic engine still yet to turn a profit.

Understanding the Media Landscape: "Must See" vs. "Must Have"

Now is the era where "must see" is replaced by "must have." To be an aficionado of entertainment one must have Netflix, yet there is not a show that demonstrably must be consumed above all others. Someone with an iPhone must have an iTunes account, even if the music selected is as eclectic as humanly possible. Younger people are urged to have social media footprints, even if that means Facebook and Twitter for some while being Instagram and Snapchat for others. Put simply, the dynamics changed where the consumption escalated while the mass consumption of any singular product dissipated. The fragmentation of American entertainment unfolded and did so rapidly.

Is there any mass left in the world of entertainment?

By the end of 2018, half of the top ten most-watched films (*Black Panther, Avengers: Infinity War, Deadpool 2, Ant Man and the Wasp, Venom*) were from the Marvel superhero genre (Li, 2018). The other five contained actors who were part of the Marvel universe, having appeared in previous Marvel film offerings. Marvel remains must-see, but the reason such superhero films seem more salient than ever is because they are, quite literally, among the very few films that qualify as blockbusters. Most everything else moved to a specific audience, not a general one.

As is the case with entertainment as we embark upon the third decade of the 21st Century. We now live in an era where Google searches become smarter based on collective, common threads of intelligence—and yet one of every six of these searches is unique, having not been typed in that exact order with those exact words ever before (Galloway, 2017). The ramifications of this fragmented landscape will be explored in subsequent chapters, most notably differentiating between common touchstones and common experiences.

References

Anderson, C. (2006). *The long tail: Why the future of business is selling less of more.* New York: Hyperion.

Billboard Staff (2018, June 6). Summer songs, 1958–2017: The top ten tunes of each summer. Retrieved on March 24, 2020 at: https://www.billboard.com/articles/news/513524/summer-songs-1985-present-top-10-tunes-each-summer-listen.

Burton, T. I. (2017, Sept. 27). Football really is America's religion. That's what made the NFL protests so powerful. *Vox.* Retrieved on March 24, 2020 at: https://www.vox.com/identities/2017/9/27/16308792/football-america-religion-nfl-protests-powerful.

Byers, D. (2015, July 10). Cruz campaign: *New York Times* is lying about bulk book sales. *Politico.* Retrieved on March 24, 2020 at: https://www.politico.com/blogs/media/2015/07/cruz-campaign-new-york-times-is-lying-about-bulk-book-sales-210318.

Del Rey, J. (2018, Apr. 7). What Amazon Prime's 100 million milestone doesn't show: The battle to keep growing in the U.S. *Recode.* Retrieved on March 24, 2020 at: https://www.recode.net/2018/4/19/17256410/amazon-prime-100-million-members-us-penetration-low-income-households-jeff-bezos.

deMoraes, L., & Hipes, P. (2018, May 22). 2017–2018 TV series rankings: NFL football, 'Big Bang' top charts. *Deadline.* Retrieved on March 24, 2020 at: https://deadline.com/2018/05/2017-2018-tv-series-ratings-rankings-full-list-of-shows-1202395851/.

Eastman, S. T., & Ferguson, D. A. (2012). *Media programming: Strategies and practices.* Boston, MA: Wadsworth.

Fisher, N. (2019, Dec. 4). Psychological research explains why TV viewing is higher than ever. *Forbes.* Retrieved on March 24, 2020 at: https://www.forbes.com/sites/nicolefisher/2019/12/04/psychological-research-explains-why-tv-viewing-is-higher-than-ever/#199a5fd83b0b.

Fottrell, Q. (2018, Aug. 4). People are spending most of their waking hours staring at screens. *Market Watch*. Retrieved on March 24, 2020 at: https://www.marketwatch.com/story/people-arespending-most-of-their-waking-hours-staring-at-screens-2018-08-01.

Gaines, C. (2017, Mar. 7). Cable and satellite TV customers pay more than $9.00 per month for ESPN networks whether they watch them or not. *Business Insider*. Retrieved on March 24, 2020 at: https://www.businessinsider.com/cable-satellite-tv-sub-fees-espn-networks-2017-3.

Galloway, S. (2017). *The four: The hidden DNA of Amazon, Apple, Facebook, and Google*. New York: Penguin.

Hawkins, D. (2018, Mar. 14). What made Hawking's 'A Brief History of Time' so popular? *The Washington Post*. Retrieved on March 24, 2020 at: https://www.washingtonpost.com/news/morning-mix/wp/2018/03/14/what-made-hawkings-a-brief-history-of-time-so-immensely-popular/?utm_term=.3d4b066730a9.

Heisler, Y. (2016, Mar. 4). Three reasons why Netflix doesn't release ratings for its original programming. *BGR*. Retrieved on March 24, 2020 at: https://bgr.com/2016/03/04/netflix-ratings-original programming/.

Hogan, M. (2018, May 2). Billboard charts change to count paid streams more than free. *Pitchfork*. Retrieved on March 24, 2020 at: https://pitchfork.com/news/billboard-charts-change-to-count-paid-streams-more-than-free/.

Holloway, D. (2018, Apr. 13). NBA regular-season ratings hit 4-year high. Retrieved on March 24, 2020 at: https://variety.com/2018/tv/news/nba-ratings-1202752848/.

Jenner, M. (2016). Is this TVIV?: On Netflix, TV III, and binge watching. *New Media & Society*, *18*(2), 257–273.

Kastrenakes, J. (2017, May 4). Most US households have given up landlines for cellphones. *The Verge*. Retrieved on March 24, 2020 at: https://www.theverge.com/2017/5/4/15544596/american-households-now-use-cellphones-more-than-landlines.

Kelleher, K. (2018, Nov. 19). It's official: Once mighty FAANG stocks have all entered a bear market. *Fortune*. Retrieved on March 24, 2020 at: http://fortune.com/2018/11/19/faang-stocks-entered-bear-market/.

Koblin, J. (2018, May 29). After racist tweet, Roseanne Barr's show is cancelled by ABC. *The New York Times*. Retrieved on March 24, 2020 at: https://www.nytimes.com/2018/05/29/business/media/roseanne-barr-offensive-tweets.html.

Li, S. (2018, Dec. 14/21). Marvel-ous box office. *Entertainment Weekly*, *29*, p. 20.

McAlone, N. (2017, Apr. 15). 55% of Americans have Netflix, but rival Amazon is closer than you might think. *Business Insider*. Retrieved on March 24, 2020 at: https://www.businessinsider.com/percent-of-americans-who-watch-netflix-amazon-youtube-2017-4.

MerchDope.com (2018). 37 mind-blowing facts, figures, and statistics—2018. Retrieved on March 24, 2020 at: https://merchdope.com/youtube-stats/.

Momoh, O. (2018, Mar. 28). FAANG stocks. *Investopedia*. Retrieved on March 24, 2020 at: https://www.investopedia.com/terms/f/faang-stocks.asp.

Moore, G. E. (1965). Cramming more components onto integrated circuits. *Electronics*, *38*(8). Retrieved at: https://drive.google.com/file/d/0By83v5TWkGjvQkpBcXJKT1I1TTA/view.

Navin, J. (2018, Sept. 7). Examining the Facebook and Netflix price charts: Is FAANG still bulletproof? *Forbes*. Retrieved on March 24, 2020 at: https://www.forbes.com/sites/john-navin/2018/09/07/examining-the-facebook-and-netflix-price-charts-is-faang-still-bullet-proof/#3e5b6d80337e.

Nielsen Insights (2014, May 6). Changing channels: Americans view just 17 channels despite record number to choose from. *Nielsen Insights*. Retrieved on March 24, 2020 at: https://www.nielsen.com/us/en/insights/news/2014/changing-channels-americans-view-just-17-channels-despite-record-number-to-choose-from.html.

Novy-Williams, E. (2017, July 12). NFL teams split record $7.8 billion in 2016, up ten percent. *Bloomberg*. Retrieved on March 24, 2020 at: https://www.bloomberg.com/news/articles/2017-07-12/nfl-teams-split-record-7-8-billion-in-2016-up-10-percent.

Otterson, J. (2018, Feb. 5). TV ratings: Super Bowl LII slips 7% from 2017 to 103.4 million viewers. *Variety*. Retrieved on March 24, 2020 at: https://variety.com/2018/tv/news/super-bowl-lii-ratings-1202687239/.

Petski, D. (2018a, Oct. 29). 'Heathers' episodes pulling following Pittsburgh synagogue shooting. *The Hollywood Reporter*. Retrieved on March 24, 2020 at: https://deadline.com/2018/10/heathers-episodes-pulled-following-synagogue-shooting-pittsburgh-1202491469/.

Petski, D. (2018b, Feb. 28). 'Heathers' reboot delayed following Parkland shooting. *The Hollywood Reporter*. Retrieved on March 24, 2020 at: https://deadline.com/2018/02/heathers-reboot-delayed-parkland-shooting-paramount-network-1202306161/.

Resnikoff, P. (2018, July 21). Drake's 'Scorpion' is the lowest selling #1 album in 27 years. *Digital Music News*. Retrieved on March 24, 2020 at: https://www.digitalmusicnews.com/2018/07/21/drake-scorpion-lowest-selling-no-1-album/.

Silver, N. (2012). *The signal and the noise: Why so many predictions fail—and some don't*. New York: Penguin.

Smith, G. (2018, Aug. 8). Who killed the great American cable-TV bundle? *Bloomberg*. Retrieved on March 24, 2020 at: https://www.bloomberg.com/news/features/2018-08-08/who-killed-the-great-american-cable-tv-bundle.

Spangler, T. (2018, Feb. 27). Netflix eyeing total of about 700 original shows in 2018. *Variety*. Retrieved on March 24, 2020 at: https://variety.com/2018/digital/news/netflix-700-original-series-2018-1202711940/.

Traina, D. (2018, June 7). Traina thoughts: Ratings for ESPN's Sunday night baseball are downright ugly. Retrieved on March 24, 2020 at: https://www.si.com/extra-mustard/2018/06/07/espn-sunday-night-baseball-ratings-decline-2018-alex-rodriguez.

Webb, A. (2019). *The big nine: How the tech titans & their thinking machines could warp humanity*. New York: Public Affairs.

Webster, J., & Ksiazek, T. B. (2012). The dynamics of audience fragmentation: Public attention in an age of digital media. *Journal of Communication*, *62*(1), 39–56.

CHAPTER FOUR

The Customization of America: My Reality Is Not Yours

In July 2017, an exceedingly popular game was released to the masses. It was distinctive in its design, but what made it really stand out from most of its other competitors was its business model. Following the earlier massive success of Riot Games' *League of Legends*, Epic Games offered their online video game entry, *Fortnite*, free of charge—and with no potential mechanism for purchasing upgrades to enhance a player's game performance. The model was stunningly successful. At its late 2018 peak, 78 million players were logging in each month, with as many as 8.3 million playing concurrently (Rodriguez, 2018). Moreover, *Fortnite* was outpacing any other online game financially, all while maintaining its free-to-purchase, "no purchases can enhance performance" principles. Rather, the money was made entirely on customizing one's own player or experience, buying V-Bucks for roughly one cent each. Those purchases added up, earning the company a reported $318 million each month (Molla, 2018). When comparing to other viral gaming options, *Fortnite* would earn more than *Pokémon Go* ($2B in total earnings) in less than seven months and could surpass *Candy Crush* ($5B in total earnings) in less than a year and a half (Ball, 2019), all accomplished through customization—the desire to have the game personalized for one's optimal consumption.

Much of this book thus far has been on the wide array of choices that collectively can micro-target one's interests to the point that, if not trying to match the media tastes of other friends and family members in the room at the same time, one can avoid undesirable media. This chapter pertains to making media content more palatable via customization, making a media platform that may initially seem neutrally valanced (perhaps one's initial experience with *Fortnite*) and make it positively valanced (via customization of content to best match one's interests). Even more than that, though, is the notion that we can custom-fit our media to create our own reality—sometimes with debilitating or even dangerous results. For instance, when a woman admits to CNN, several months after the release of the Mueller Report related to the degree of Donald Trump's involvement in Russian interference in the 2016 election, that she had never heard anything negative about Trump existed in the report because she watched almost exclusively conservative media (Drum, 2019), the bubble one creates can be as personal as it is limiting. This chapter will first, focus on the filtering and aggregating of algorithms that provide personalized realities in media (the creation of the bubble) before then delving into the manner to which one can person personalize media to best fit one's desires (the customization of the bubble.)

The Era of Ubiquitous Choice

Both the Arby's restaurant slogan ("different is good") and Apple, Inc. mantra ("think different") was a harbinger for the optimization of America, making the slogan paramount to the notion that "options are good". After all, who would not want more options? Options are good, representing freedom and choice; restrictions are bad, representing limitations and confinement. Indeed, we are not using this book to argue that the options are inherently bad, but that options cannot be equated with better options—and media that gives us what we desire should not be equated as being inherently superior media. We are not claiming the need for a sequel to Bruce Springsteen's 1992 song "57 Channels and Nothing On" where there now thousands of media channels fitting that description. There is a ton of quality content readily "on". On the list of Rotten Tomatoes' top 100 best-reviewed films of 2018, even #98, the documentary film *Dark Money*, has 95% "fresh"/positive reviews. Youth aged 18–24 spend 3.2 hours per day using mobile applications ("The 2017 Mobile App Report", 2017), presumably not because they find the choices limiting, frustrating, or unfulfilling.

And yet … those choices can be debilitating. Information overload lead to a form of analysis paralysis with a dizzying array of choice. Consider Schwartz's Paradox of Choice where there is a point, relatively early on within the selection process, in which one determines that a search is "good enough" and opts to decide upon a "winner," whether that is an Amazon purchase, Google search, or Netflix viewing option. As Schwartz (2004) explains, choices expand to personalize and specialize decisions and desires; choices exist to provide not just what we want, but what we *really* want. However, Schwartz explains how such vast options can be contradictory to happiness, precisely because one's specialized selections are inherently isolating (when there are over 100 flavors of ice cream, it is difficult to find someone who loves your #1 option of Moon Mist flavor in the freezer). Moreover, the greater number of selections, the more one will believe there is a risk of choosing the "wrong" one; if selecting a potential mate, the dizzying array of ways to connect via media show that someone potentially, quite literally, a touch of a finger away. Thus, marriage becomes one of the last markers of adulthood, rather than one of the first as it was in decades past (Rabin, 2018).

One of the most prevalent sayings in modern society goes that "it is good to have options," yet studies are finding that there is a limit to the truth in this axiom. Explaining everything from the consumer who spends two hours at the grocery store to then ultimately still qualify for the "ten items or under" express line to the person who holds up the timing of drive-thru line, Reutskaja, Lindner, Nagel, Andersen, and Camerer (2018) find that the ideal number of options was less than 24 and more than six, indicating that 12 was a fairly good compromise when determining the optimal number of choices to make a useful selection without analysis paralysis setting in. Still, what is one to do in a media environment in which the choices truly are undefinable?

We are now reaching the point that differences between ubiquity and infinity are essentially blurred without distinction. There is no practical difference between a Google search yielding 45,000 results and one yielding 45 million results when 71% of the websites visited are among the top 10 offered on page 1 (Jacobson, 2017). Similarly, there are platforms where ubiquity and infinity might as well be the same thing; the 40 million songs available on iTunes or Spotify might as well be limitless—no one could feasibly listen to them all even once within a single lifetime.

Yet, the psychological distinction between plentiful options and unlimited options is worthy of note. A useful exemplar is offered in the study by Ariely (2010), who offered subjects two different types of candy for purchase: a Hershey's kiss (a functionally sound selection) for one cent and a Lindt chocolate truffle (which most would find to be a superior/more decadent selection) for 26 cents. A majority (60%) opted for the Lindt chocolate, presumably with the reason that if one were to pay a small amount for a treat, it may as well be for the better of the two options. However, when the price was reduced by a single cent (free for the Hershey's kiss and 25 cents for the Lindt chocolates), the results shifted dramatically, with a clear majority now preferring the Hershey's kiss. The value of free represented limitless possibilities—abundance, quite literally, without measure (Anderson, 2010). Businesses now cater to the concept, from endless appetizers at the local TGI Fridays to the unlimited data plans for most cell carriers. Such corporations know the appeal of unlimited possibility and profit from the fact that limits of time and space still make any of these less reasonable for one to pursue. The modern health club is the classic example; each January health club membership applications spike by roughly 40% (Swanson, 2016), where New Year's Resolutions form aspirations of exercise, weight loss, and healthier lifestyle. The unlimited access to these clubs is the appeal; the lack of free time, willpower, and desire to make exercise a top priority is how such companies make money. However, both ubiquity and customization have the same natural enemy: Father Time. There is no advent that changes the 24-hour day and the need to eat, sleep, and perform all of the other things that life requires. Thus, we must make decisions, which can beget our own, unique existence that looks quite different than the mediated worlds of others.

Choose Your Own Reality: The Optics of Modern Metrics

Choose your own adventure narratives had been around for decades, yet on December 28, 2018, the Netflix series *Black Mirror* upped the ante considerably. With an episode dubbed "Black Mirror: Bandersnatch", a truly interactive episode was released—one that would go on to win the Emmy Award for Best Television Movie. From deciding cereal brands to music choices to the amount of information to disclose to the lead character's therapist, viewers were able to shape their own experiences. Netflix even tracked how people customized their storyline within "Black Mirror: Bandersnatch" revealing part of the audience psyche in the process (Gardner, 2019). On a more holistic level, such media products change the equation from the usual binary notion of "have you seen X?" Indeed, this episode of *Black Mirror* had people watching multiple times to discover alternate endings, plot twists, and hidden content "Easter eggs" as most experienced the episode in less than an hour from beginning to end, yet there was over five hours of content which could be included, depending on the plot tree of viewer choice (Bui, 2018).

Such customized episode contexts underscore the bubbles in which many now gladly reside (often.) My reality is not your reality. What trends for me does not trend for you. The moment you click on a single YouTube video, your suggested videos are inextricably different than someone else. The first time you rate a film on Netflix, the generated suggestions are different for you than others. Each selection represents a new permutation. Each permutation takes a person a step toward customization and a step away from mass consumption and shared experiences. Media psychologists tell us the ability to personalize one's media content palate has considerable appeal (Kalyanaraman & Sundar, 2006), yet diffuses even the most popular of our content choices into slivers of shared reality fused with personalized elements of interest.

A prime example of how something with massive metrics nonetheless features considerable customization comes in the form of the 2019 music smash, *Old Town Road*—whose metrics (19+ weeks at #1) make it the *biggest song in recorded history* (Frank, 2019). Recorded by previously-unknown musician Lil Nas X, the song was as eclectic (the video featured the Black gay rapper on horseback) as it was confounding (initially featured on Billboard's Country charts before being realigned as exclusively an R&B/Hip Hop entry; Leight, 2019). Even more peculiar, *Old Town Road* benefited from chart decisions that combined remixes into one single entry; the song had five official remixed versions, including ones from country music's Billy Ray Cyrus, DJ Diplo, rapper Young Thug combined with 12-year-old yodeler/singer Mason Ramsey, and K-Pop megaband BTS. All metrics for each song formed an *Old Town Road* juggernaut that rewrote the Billboard singles history books.

And yet … this megahit never led the radio airplay charts for even one week. Not one. Billboard's metrics included downloads (which buoyed the song as fans could purchase it not just once, but six separate times) and streams (which are a faulty metric given their ability to be manipulated; Smirke, 2019). All of which is to say that while *Old Town Road* was, undoubtedly, a viral hit, customization and the fragmentation of music industry measurement preclude one's ability to understand the magnitude in which this hit unfolded. As Bruner and Chow (2019) explained, "the song became less a single record and more a fluid canvas for transgression" (p. 67).

Of course, any perceived harm or problem arising from customization is negligible when the stakes are determining which form of a *Black Mirror* episode was viewed or whether *Old Town Road* should be placed above previous record holders *One Sweet Day* (Mariah Carey and Boys II Men) and *Despacito* (Luis Fonsi featuring Daddy Yankee and Justin Bieber) atop the pantheon of most popular hit singles. Nevertheless, the detriments of such customizable media crystallize when one the customizations move from soft entertainment to hard news.

As mentioned earlier in this book, earlier iterations of news necessitated gatekeeping practices. The limited amount of space in a newspaper allowed the publication of "only the news that is fit to print"; the 22 minutes (once allowing for commercials) within an evening news telecast required substantial editing and decisions to forego telling interesting and/or intriguing stories that might not be deemed the most imperative of the day. In such an environment, agenda-setting theory (McCombs & Shaw, 1972) moved to the forefront of much news media scholarship as it represented a clear movement behind faulty hypodermic needle theories to a more realistic sense of the influence of media, claiming that media could not overtly tell people what to think, but could be quite effective in telling people where to focus one's attention. Framing theory (Goffman, 1974) then forged new pathways into the manner in which such content is advanced with Gitlin (1980) adopting Goffman's schema of interpretation to contend that media-oriented "frames are persistent patterns of cognition, interpretation, and presentation, of selection, emphasis, and exclusion, by which symbol-handlers routinely organized discourse, whether verbal or visual" (p. 7).

These theories proved useful as America moved into the 1980s and choices became much more expansive than before. For instance, in 1982 Ted Turner's Cable News Network (CNN) launched an ancillary channel, CNN2 (later to become CNN Headline News, which then became HLN in 2008) based on a simple yet ambitious prospect: repeating the equivalent of the evening news, 48 times per day. With the tagline "around the world in 30 minutes", Headline News became a staple of efficient news dissemination; one need not worry if they joined the broadcast at the top or the bottom of the hour as they could be assured that, after 30 minutes, they would have witnessed what the channel current had to offer.

Soon news channels would differentiate not just on programming optics but also on the brands in which stories were shown—and even if stories were highlighted at all. By the turn of the century, grounds were largely defined on the brands in which they occupied, with FOX News contending to be "fair and balanced" while occupying more conservative talking points and MSNBC ultimately finding room to grow an audience based on the liberal counterprogramming to the FOX News agenda. Each brand was customized for a given audience member at home; after 9/11, FOX hosts donned American flag pins to symbolize national solidarity while other networks finding the practice unethical, fearful of seeming biased in the rendering of war-related coverage (Caffier, 2019).

Even the notion of the time of day became customized for such news outlets to the point that a message is crafted for the individual audience member. MSNBC was hosted predominantly by liberal hosts in the evening, yet was flanked by a morning show, *Morning Joe*, that was named after its conservative host, Joe Scarborough. FOX News contended that they were a news agency during the daytime hours, yet not so in the evening where their hosts were not "journalists" but, rather, "personalities." The distinction has become even more parsed, with FOX News host Sean Hannity agreeing that he is not a journalist, but insisting that his eponymous show, *Hannity*, "does journalism" (Mazza, 2019, para. 1).

News networks are clear examples of media customization, yet other networks (and forms of media) exemplify this to a lesser degree. Television channels, following ESPN's lead in finding that VCR's (and later digital video recorders [DVR's]) would diminish their advertising dollars unless a brand was established to justify hikes in monthly subscription fees (see Miller & Shales, 2011), determined that brands must be niches that cater to more precise audiences. To wit, billionaire Ted Turner owned successful networks in TBS (dubbed the "Superstation") and TNT, yet discovered both networks lacked the defined identity needed to justify viewer loyalty in a customized age. Hence, programs shifted space and syndicated choices begat two new labels in 2004: TBS: Very funny and TNT: We Know Drama.

Networks were evolving rapidly to respond to the changing models, readily shifting brands. The Nashville Network (established 1983) was deemed too regional, becoming TNN in 2000, which was then too bland, which then became Spike in 2003, which then would need to hew closer to the media conglomerate that owned it to become the Paramount Network that it was at the time of this writing. Sci-Fi would eventually become Syfy because the former was a genre but the latter was a brand. The Learning Channel had already been changed to TLC to make it less obviously about learning, but soon the brand became about a different type of TLC, with a slogan contending that "everyone needs a little" [tender, loving care] TLC along with programs such as *Here Comes Honey Boo* and *Dr. Pimple Popper*.

Once streaming entered the equation, programs that were not successful in one location found that a change in brand could bolster their audience. While this had been done plenty of times before even in pre-cable eras, streaming could make a previous season a hit which would then bolster a current season on a different network (witness AMC's *Breaking Bad* and CW's *Riverdale* with ratings spikes in later seasons that are largely attributed to Netflix). The results became increasingly extreme; *YOU* averaged 1.1 million viewers a week when it premiered on Lifetime; the same first-season episodes found 40 million subscriber views *in one month* on Netflix (Agard, 2019).

The end result: most concurred that "the definition of television entertainment is changing, and it now means different things to different people" (Lachapelle, 2019, para. 1). The same could be advanced for virtually every media platform and device. The game has changed so much that it is difficult to determine who and/or what is your primary media consumption competitor. When such media options become niche, the audiences concerning them become more homogenous. This situation becomes valuable for advertising and other marketing elements seeking certain demographics as now, they truly can find them.

The Increasing Relevance of Niche Gratification Theory

In prior decades, question pertained as to whether a device or service was worth one's time and attention: Is this newspaper worth the subscription rate? Do I watch enough television to justify the cable subscription? Those decisions, while important, represented a series of relatively linear, simple choices based on theoretical assumptions of uses and gratifications (Blumler & Katz, 1974), where the consumer becomes an active participant (see Bryant & Miron, 2004) in media selection to fulfill desired needs and obtain varying levels of gratification. However, when choices became even more plentiful, Anderson's (2006) conception of the long tail formed around the notion that niches could extend forever to the point that hits are not as important as a long series of smaller successes. Niche gratification theory (Dimmick, 2003) focuses on precisely these choices to explain why people opt (or not) to invest resources (time or money) to a media selection. Sometimes these selections have prongs: a book that is worthy of reading from the local library may not be "shelf-worthy" on one's own bookcase at home; a Hulu subscription might be worth an occasional one-month purchase, but not provide enough content to warrant a year-long investment. The type of content, combined with the time it takes to procure/consume a media product and the physical space it requires to have access to it combine to form a reason why a new medium, platform, or service succeeds or fails (Dimmick, Chen, & Li, 2004). The default mindset becomes the old media; one does not upgrade their smartphone unless the new media promises to be significantly better. The established media offering, thus, works to avoid exclusion and extinction (Dimmick, Klein, & Stafford, 2000) by either adapting or doubling down on what it offers that is unique or simpler. Consider a media conglomerate like the National Broadcasting Company (NBC). NBC, witnessing the success of reruns of shows such as *The Office* or *Parks and Recreation* on Netflix, could adapt to a changing streaming marketplace by removing them from the competitor and providing its own streaming service (as it has with the April 2020 release of Peacock). Divergently, it could also reiterate what it provides that other streaming services lack, such as exclusive access to live sports like Sunday Night Football or the Olympics. Either way, the industry stalwart can survive and even thrive if consumers feel either of these prospects are viable. Viability is then defined differently in the age of customization, a world in which something reaching one million people could be economically prosperous while something with ten times the reach might be disastrous. Such decisions are based on an increasingly relevant principle in the media world known as narrowcasting.

Enter: Narrowcasting

Moore's Law, based on the premise that the rate of technological capacity roughly doubles every two years (Moore, 1965), has placed such production abilities in hyperdrive, once such technologies were reaching exponential levels. An ancillary of Moore's Law, Edholm's Law (Cherry, 2004) pertains to the same rate of bandwidth offered in mass media specifically, with the result being the widest array of content ever offered with a population that is doubling only every X years, not every two.

The response to the confluence of a relatively stagnant population size to a massively expanding media offering universe was niche programming, shorthanded as "narrowcasting." One would think that such a term would be a byproduct of the mobile digital era, but such an assumption would be wrong. The term was first known to be employed in 1967 by public broadcasting supporter J.C.R. Licklider, who predicted "a multiplicity of television networks aimed at serving the needs of smaller, specialized audiences … I should like to coin the term 'narrowcasting,' using it to emphasize the rejection or dissolution of the constraints imposed by commitment to a monolithic mass-appeal, broadcast approach" (in Parsons, 2003). Offering a direct contrast to the concept of broadcasting, narrowcasting began to flourish as Edholm's Law took hold of an Internet based consumption society.

When the benchmark for what constitutes profitability drops, the need for wide-ranging media hits is supplanted by the desire to micro-target certain fans of certain genres. Put simply, if all of the family was not going to be watching the same thing at the same time anyway, one might as well produce content that could not only be acceptable but could also thrive for each individual family member. Considering films, for instance, barring the rare "please the whole family film" (typically now a superhero/comic book movie) family members could each stream something that is not a compromise and, instead, a selection that a single person deems to be the most optimal selection among a truly dizzying array of options.

Thus, content can be created that micro-targets the interest of, say, 14–18 year old females and, in doing so, an opportunity for marketers (Barasch & Berger, 2014) is unveiled who can, with relative precision, find their optimal audience for that high school girl's eyes to see. When daytime television in the 1980s and 1990s thrived in an era of talk shows and soap operas, advertisers targeted the stay-at-home mother with considerable acuity; now such principles are much more finely honed and applied to virtually every media offering, whether a television program, Instagram application, or podcast stream.

Customization, thus, allows micro-targeting to the point that older metrics are no longer nearly as viable. For instance, if one wished to predict the rating of a television program, until the turn of the century one variable contributed to that determination more than any other: lead-in rating (Billings, Eastman, & Newton, 1998). Over 50% of a rating was determined by what was on immediately before a program, leading to decisions like placing a marginal program like *Boston Common* on directly after a huge hit like NBC's *Friends*; it could still be a top-ten rated program simply by its wedged occupancy between *Friends* and *Seinfeld* in the coveted must-see TV lineup as the majority of people would not actively change the channel (either from a lack of perceived other options or simply not the desire to walk to the television (pre-remote control) or find the remote control to change the channel. The same would happen in other forms of media; radio stations seeking to play niche songs could get away with doing so by playing a hit song before and after as tune-in rate was way more viable than tune-out rate.

Juxtapose such principles in the age in which we now live. A website "bounce rate" is either defined by the industry as the percentage of people who leave a website within 30 seconds or, alternatively, the percentage of people who have single interaction visits on the website (Peyton, 2019). Either way, anything below 50% is deemed better than the industry average, meaning that having 40% of your audience check out your content and immediately opt out within seconds is actually an *impressive* result (Peyton, 2019). Given how people actively know what they are seeking (or at least the type of information they desire), bundling elements into a single format is less desirable. If people just want sports stories, they cancel subscriptions to the newspaper (which bundles its sports with local news, classifieds, etc.) and either read single online stories or place their money into a subscription service like *The Athletic* (all sports, all the time.)

Changing Counting Metrics: A Music Case Study

Hence, the unit of analysis in which most forms of media are measured is altered to bend to a customized world. Newspaper circulation is replaced by number of clicks to an article. Television viewership moves from being measured in live metrics to live plus seven day metrics. DVD sales become less relevant than number of streams. When these units of analyses change, industries can adapt, yet some find the measurements for exposure are different than the measurements needed to attain economic success.

Consider the music industry. For many decades, the unit of analysis was the album. Yes, one could buy a single, but it was the unit price of the album that made all of the difference. At the time of this writing, in the history of recorded music, ten albums have sold more than 40 million copies, as Table 4.1 highlights:

Table 4.1. Best Selling Albums of All-Time

Artist	Album	Year	Unit Sales (millions)
Michael Jackson	*Thriller*	1982	66
Eagles	*Greatest Hits (1971–1975)*	1976	51
AC/DC	*Back in Black*	1980	50
Pink Floyd	*The Dark Side of the Moon*	1973	45
Whitney Houston/ Various	*The Bodyguard*	1992	45
Meat Loaf	*Bat Out of Hell*	1977	43
Eagles	*Hotel California*	1976	42
Bee Gees/Various	*Saturday Night Fever*	1977	40
Fleetwood Mac	*Rumours*	1977	40
Shania Twain	*Come On Over*	1997	40

As one can witness, none of these albums has been released since the turn of the 21st Century. Of course, one could claim such a list is a byproduct of lagging indicators; *Thriller* (1982) has had nearly four decades to amass its 66 million in sales whereas Beyoncé's *Lemonade* (2016) has had substantially less time to do so, with current sales of 2.5 million. Still, 74 albums have sold at least 20 million units, and only three (Eminem's *The Eminem Show*, 2002; Norah Jones' *Come Away With Me*, 2002; Adele's *25*, 2015) were released after January 9, 2001, the date iTunes was released to the public and the unit of analysis changed to the single.

The appeal of the music single was self-evident. Rather than listening to an entire album of songs that could range from the highly appealing to the forgettable, iTunes (and the many formats that it spurred) could easily allow a person to assemble a customized playlist for roughly the same cost (sometimes far less once Napster and other streaming services allowed similar features). This was quite a boon for the consumer, whose desire for music had never waned, but it turned an entire industry upside down.

In previous decades, musicians made the large majority of their money from sales, largely album sales, with singles contributing a much smaller amount. Live performances could even be loss leaders; you toured to sell the album. However, the customizable music consumption industry flips that equation. An album selling on iTunes for $9.99 distributes those dollars in a manner that does not prioritize the artist (Investing Answers, 2019), as Figure 4.1 shows.

Dollars

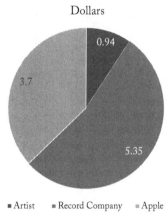

■ Artist ■ Record Company ■ Apple

Figure 4.1. Distributions of a $9.99 iTunes Album Sale

As one can see, selling a million albums (quite a feat in today's modern age) does not make an artist a millionaire, but does manage to put $3.7 million in Apple's pocket for facilitating that sale via iTunes. We are merely picking on Apple; virtually all modern forms of music distribution function the same way. Spotify can compensate the "holder" of a song as little as $0.006 per stream (Sehgal, 2018), with the "holder" constituting many entities beyond the artist, including the label, producers, etc. A million streams on Pandora yields $1,650 (Castillo, 2015), again to be distributed around a wide variety of interested parties. The result, argues Sehgal (2018) is that while there used to be "a glimmer of hope that a musician could earn a decent income on sales" musicians now are "essentially giving away their music in return for pennies" (para. 6).

Thus, touring becomes a priority. Part of this comes from a lack of proper funding in the sales model; part also arises from the premises of this book: we love customization, yet still crave the communal, shared experience. As *Rockonomics* author Alan Krueger (2019) asserts: "No longer is the focus just on the music. Concerts and festivals sell experiences" (p. 11)—and those experiences are not cheap. Concert ticket prices rose sharply, from five dollars back in the late 1970s when all of those 40 million plus-selling albums were being produced to an average ticket price of $94.31 in 2018 (Statista, 2019); the cost of a concert has risen 250% faster than the rate of inflation (Krueger, 2019). But then consider the top-grossing concerts of all time (as reported by Ellison, 2018):

Table 4.2. Top 10 Highest Grossing Tours of All-Time (Ellison, 2018)

Artist	Tour	Years	Gross ($/Millions)
U2	*360 Degrees*	2009–2011	736.4
Guns and Roses	*Not in this Lifetime*	2016–2018	563.3
The Rolling Stones	*A Bigger Bang*	2005–2007	558.3
Ed Sheeran	*Divide*	2017–2019	551.3
Coldplay	*A Head Full of Dreams*	2016–2017	523.0
Roger Waters	*The Wall: Live*	2010–2013	458.6
AC/DC	*Black Ice*	2008–2010	448.6
Madonna	*Sticky & Sweet*	2008–2009	408
U2	*Vertigo*	2005–2006	389
Garth Brooks/ Trisha Yearwood	*World Tour*	2004–2007	364.3

The first thing one notices is that all have happened in the post-iTunes era where concerts became revenue drivers and sales became negligible economic factors. The second thing one might notice would be that most of the artists are products of a different era. While Ed Sheeran and Coldplay make the list, they are exceptions to the rule. Most, including the Rolling Stones, U2, and Madonna, are byproducts of the *album* era. Concerts become where all major artists make the majority of their money; even "The Boss" is not exempt: Bruce Springsteen now has concerts as *96 percent* of his overall revenue stream (Christman, 2018). The music economy changed, and while Post Malone and Drake are top stream-ing options, an eighties band with a musician named Slash can top them on the concert circuit, even more than 25 years after Guns and Roses' last top 10 single. Arguments could be advanced on a number of fronts, yet perhaps this pre-mium price on nostalgia occurs because people's knowledge of these artists run deeper; fans listened to such 1970s and 1980s artists in clusters (albums), rather than amalgamated playlists with other popular artists of today. Such trends have long been predicted by those within the music industry. As David Bowie once summarized:

> Music itself is going to become like running water or electricity ... You'd better be prepared for doing a lot of touring because that's really the only unique situation that's going to be left. It's terribly exciting ... But on the other hand it doesn't matter if you think it's exciting or not; it's what's going to happen. (in Krueger, 2019, p. 19)

Customized News, Partitioned Realities

The drawbacks of customization are relatively negligible, though, when compared to the manner in which we customize our media-based learning. Yes, not sharing a common experience of a television finale or Beyoncé album might cause less communal sharing, but problems loom larger when one cannot even agree on core tenets of reality. Debates cannot occur and compromises cannot be articulated when two sides fail to have basic understandings of the same issues. Reverting to the quote in our introduction from Senator Patrick Moynihan ("Everyone is entitled to their own opinions, but they are not entitled to their own facts"), there may be media outlets—and consumers of those outlets—who counter with the question: are you so *sure* about that?

Through vast networks of shared, established connections, one fulfills a variety of social needs. However, a process Couldry and Mejias (2019) dub data colonialism exacts economic interests to the desires each person exhibits. Not surprisingly, the Freudian pleasure principle quickly is facilitated in the realm of how we seek and consume our news as (cognizant or not), people make media decisions to maximize pleasure and avoid pain. When there were relatively few news outlets, this largely became a binary of *whether* one would seek out news; if a person liked a politician who was experiencing a negative news cycle, supporters would likely watch less news or avoid it altogether for a segment of time. They were aware negative news existed and, consistent with uses and gratifications principles as well (see Blumler & McQuail, 1969), they were motivated to consume other things that would bring them greater satisfaction.

In modern news cycles, the notion of whether one seeks news is largely replaced by the *type* of news one seeks—not just the content, but the overall *valence* of that content. Toff and Neilsen (2018, p. 636), utilized "distributed discovery", the proportion of extreme news avoiders, finding that this proportion is in the single-digits—roughly 2–8% according to Toff (in Black, 2019). For those mere infrequent news seekers, three categories largely percolate depending upon the degree to which one wishes to customize their news: "news finds me", "the information is out there" and "I don't know what to believe" (Toff & Neilsen, 2018). Enter customization.

For those ascribing to the "news finds me" proposition, what inevitably will percolate within ones' stream of news (whether social media feeds or other elements of commonly trod media options), will be what others deem to be worthy of consumption. Put simply, the most popular will survive. The problem inherent in such a grouping arises from Levine's (2014, 2020) conception of truth-default theory, where the underlying assumption of any piece of information is that it is true and largely unfiltered. Akin to the concept of "innocent until proven guilty", information is, thus, vetted in that same manner: non-deceptive unless proven otherwise. Truth-default theory assumes a media source has some veracity ("why else would it be popular enough to find me?"), but neglecting the capitalistic premise in which much information is now advanced: there is more to be gained, both in terms of social and economic capital, on the customized micro-group than the generalized macro-group.

Those who customize their news based on the premise that "the information is out there" function within in an environment in which hyperpartisan news and other forms of slant or bias represent a third wave of selective exposure research (Barnidge & Peacock, 2019). The problem with this form of customizable news is the presumption that the reader/consumer has ample media literacy skills. Quite often, unfortunately, that is not the case as spreadable media (see Jenkins, Ford, & Green, 2013) works often in direct contrast with media literacy to create what Mihailidis and Viotty (2017) dub a "post-fact" society (p. 441). The information is, indeed, out there, yet it is mingled with many other clones and facsimiles that appear to be conspicuously like news yet are not, either in forms of objectivity or, more problematically, substantiation.

Finally, the "I don't know what to believe" mindset features the justifiably skeptical news consumer (Jang & Kim, 2018) who nonetheless feels helpless to be able to customize an informed tableau of media information options. Even if Pennycook and Rand (2019) successfully advance that lack of reasoning (as opposed to motivated reasoning) is the best explanation of the stickiness of fake news, one cannot automatically assume that those questioning every form of information rate any higher on reasoning functions. Rather, the analysis paralysis reported in the previously mentioned study from Reutskaja et al. (2018) arises again here as the range of options and possible placements on the spectrum from accurate to fictional proves too much for many to overcome. In the end, "I don't know what to believe" consumers often throw their hands up in despair, opting to customize a different form of their media world where the stakes are not quite as high—say a Spotify playlist or sport-based Twitter feed.

What Customization Hath Wrought

The negatives of media customization indeed range from the plummeting financial prospects of music royalties to the dangerous ramifications of a public defined less from news they can substantiate and more about news they can enjoy. However, this is not to conclude that customization is a net negative on the overall ecosystem of media options. Decreased media costs allow all of these options to exist in a manner never before witnessed. From book self-publishing to the ability to advance journalism via web-based mechanisms with little physical infrastructure, the margins of the consumption curve are filled, yet in areas in which margins did not exist before. Even within magazines, an industry regarded as in the decline, the number of magazines in U.S. circulation rose from 5,340 in 2002 to 7,218 in 2018 (Watson, 2019)—but the total number of magazines reaching just 1% of the population is a mere 13. Again, Anderson's (2006) long tail conception comes to the fore as a society of niches builds individual media utopias that, nonetheless, are not shared experiences or even realities.

Customization gives people choices, which bolsters gratification and enjoyment while diminishing commonality of interest. Identification with a shared media option is replaced by differentiation in which one forms their own YouTube subscription list, Nintendo Wii "Mii" or slate of Slack channels. The popularity and economic power of customization cannot be quashed. As the thirst for *Fortnite* costumes and skins continues to thrive in a market valuing individuality of play, if asked whether it is acceptable that one's experience is not directly the same as the other, more often than not that answer is offered in the affirmative, indicating that replacing commonality with customization is a trade most are willing to make.

Nevertheless, as the following chapter will show, just because an individual is comfortable not having common experiences does not mean they are willing to function without cultural barometers. When those barometers fail to materialize, willing disbelief will urge us to manufacture them in the guise of virality.

References

Agard, C. (2019, Feb. 1). The streaming effect. *Entertainment Weekly*, *30*, p. 18.

Anderson, C. (2006). *The long tail: Why the future of business is selling less of more*. New York, NY: Hatchette.

Anderson, C. (2010). *FREE: The future of a radical price*. New York, NY: Hyperion.

Ariely, D. (2010). *Predictably irrational: The hidden forces that shape our decisions*. New York, NY: Harper Perennial.

Ball, M. (2019, Feb. 5). Fortnite is the future, but probably not for the reasons you think. *Redef*. Retrieved on March 24, 2020 at: https://redef.com/original/5c599eb966c7bb710656c824.

Barasch, A. & Berger, J. (2014). Broadcasting and narrowcasting: How audience size affects what people share. *Journal of Marketing Research*, *51*(3), 286–299.

Barnidge, M., & Peacock, C. (2019). A third wave of selective exposure research?: The challenges posed by hyperpartisan news on social media. *Media and Communication*, *7*(3), 4–7.

Billings, A. C., Eastman, S. T., & Newton, G. D. (1998). Atlanta revisited: Prime-time promotion in the 1996 Olympic games. *Journal of Sport & Social Issues, 22*(1), 65–78.

Black, E. (2019, Sept. 23). Ben Toff on Americans' news consumption—from 'avoiders' to embracers. *MinnPost*. Retrieved on March 24, 2020 at: https://www.minnpost.com/eric-black-ink/2019/09/ben-toff-on-americans-news-consumption-from-avoiders-to-embracers/.

Blumler, J. G., & Katz, E. (1974). *The uses of mass communications: Current perspectives on gratifications research*. Beverly Hills, CA: Sage.

Blumler, J. G., & McQuail, D. (1969). *Television in politics: Its uses and influence*. Chicago: University of Chicago Press.

Bruner, R., & Chow, A. R. (2019, Dec. 16). Top 10 songs. *Time, 97*, p. 67.

Bryant, J., & Miron, D. (2004). Theory and research in mass communication. *Journal of Communication, 54*(4), 662–704.

Bui, H. T. (2018, Dec. 26). 'Black Mirror: Bandersnatch' will be a choose your own adventure movie with five hours of footage. *Slashfilm*. Retrieved on March 24, 2020 at: https://www.slashfilm.com/black-mirror-bandersnatch-movie/.

Caffier, J. (2019, Feb. 21). Those stupid American flag pins may finally be dying out. *Vice*. Retrieved on March 24, 2020 at: https://www.vice.com/en_us/article/7xnwnq/those-stupid-american-flag-pins-may-finally-be-dying-out.

Castillo, M. (2015, Mar. 15). Is the music streaming industry destined to leave artists unhappy? *AdWeek*. Retrieved on March 24, 2020 at: https://www.adweek.com/digital/music-streaming-industry-destined-leave-artists-unhappy-163466/.

Cherry, S. (2004). Edholm's law of bandwidth. *IEEE Spectrum, 41*(7), 58–60.

Christman, E. (2018, July 20). Billboard's 2018 money makers: 50 highest paid musicians. *Billboard*. Retrieved on March 24, 2020 at: https://www.billboard.com/photos/8520668/2018-highest-paid-musicians-money-makers.

Couldry, N. & Mejias, U. A. (2019). *The costs of connection: How data is colonizing human life and appropriating it for capitalism*. Palo Alto, CA: Stanford University Press.

Dimmick, J. (2003). *Media competition and coexistence: The theory of the niche*. Mahwah, NJ: Lawrence Erlbaum Associates.

Dimmick, J., Chen, Y., & Li, Z. (2004). Competition between the Internet and traditional news media: The gratification-opportunities niche dimension. *The Journal of Media Economics, 17*(1), 19–33.

Dimmick, J., Klein, S., & Stafford, L. (2000). The gratification niches of personal e-mail and the telephone. Competition, displacement and complementarity. *Communication Research, 27*(1), 227–248.

Drum, K. (2019, May 31). Quote of the day: The Mueller report says bad things about Trump? FOX News never mentioned that. *Mother Jones*. Retrieved on March 24, 2020 at: https://www.motherjones.com/kevin-drum/2019/05/quote-of-the-day-the-mueller-report-says-bad-things-about-trump-fox-news-never-mentioned-that/.

Ellison, E. (2018, Dec. 13). The highest grossing concert tours of all-time. *Work + Money.* Retrieved on March 24, 2020 at: https://www.workandmoney.com/s/highest-grossing-concert-tours-ed51a7b3f92c4afb.

Frank, A. (2019, July 29). 'Old Town Road' just became Billboard's longest running #1 song ever. *Vox.* Retrieved on March 24, 2020 at: https://www.vox.com/culture/2019/7/29/8937934/lil-nas-x-old-town-road-billboard-charts-record-breaking-single.

Gardner, E. (2019, Jan. 11). Netflix's 'Black Mirror: Bandersnatch' leads to 'Choose Your Own Adventure' trademark lawsuit. *The Hollywood Reporter.* Retrieved on March 20, 2020 at: https://www.hollywoodreporter.com/thr-esq/netflix-sued-exploiting-choose-your-own-adventure-black-mirror-bandersnatch-1175428

Gitlin, T. (1980). *The whole world is watching: Mass media in the making and unmaking of the new left.* Berkeley, CA: University of California Press.

Goffman, E. (1974). *Frame analysis: An essay on the organization of experience.* New York, NY: Harper & Row.

Investing Answers (2019). Who really profits from your iTunes downloads? Retrieved on March 24, 2020 at: https://investinganswers.com/articles/who-really-profits-your-itunes-downloads.

Jacobson, M. (2017, Aug. 17). How far down the search engine results page will most people go? *Leverage Marketing.* Retrieved on March 24, 2020 at: https://www.theleverageway.com/blog/how-far-down-the-search-engine-results-page-will-most-people-go/.

Jang, S. M., Kim, J. K. (2018). Third person effects of fake news: Fake news regulation and media literacy interventions. *Computers in Human Behavior, 80,* 295–302.

Jenkins, H., Ford, S., & Green, J. (2013). *Spreadable media: Creative value and meaning in a networked culture.* New York, NY: New York University Press.

Kalyanaraman, S., & Sundar, S. S. (2006). The psychological appeal of personalized content in web portals: Does customization affect attitudes and behavior? *Journal of Communication, 56*(1), 110–132.

Krueger, A. B. (2019). *Rockonomics: A backstage tour of what the music industry can teach us about economics and life.* New York, NY: Currency.

Lachapelle, T. (2019, Feb. 8). The TV industry's biggest question in 2019: What is TV, exactly? *BNN Bloomberg.* Retrieved on March 24, 2020 at: https://www.bnnbloomberg.ca/the-tv-industry-s-biggest-question-in-2019-what-is-tv-exactly-1.1211372.

Leight, E. (2019, Mar. 26). Lil Nas X's 'Old Town Road' was a country hit. Then country changed its mind. *Rolling Stone.* Retrieved on March 24, 2020 at: https://www.rollingstone.com/music/music-features/lil-nas-x-old-town-road-810844/.

Levine, T. (2014). Truth-default theory (TDT): A theory of human deception and deception detection. *Journal of Language and Social Psychology, 33*(4), 378–392.

Levine, T. (2020). *Duped: Truth-default theory and the social science of lying and deception.* Tuscaloosa, AL: University of Alabama Press.

Mazza, E. (2019, Feb. 14). Sean Hannity comes up with a new way to describe his show's 'journalism.' *The Huffington Post.* Retrieved on March 24, 2020 at: https://www.huffpost.com/entry/sean-hannity-the-whole-newspaper_n_5c651a10e4b0233af971861e.

McCombs, M., & Shaw, D. (1972). The agenda-setting function of mass media. *The Public Opinion Quarterly, 36*(2), 176–187.

Mihailidis, P., & Viotty, S. (2017). Spreadable spectacle in digital culture: Civic expression, fake news, and the role of media literacies in a 'post-fact' society. *American Behavioral Scientist, 61*(4), 441–454.

Miller, J. A., & Shales, T. (2011). *Those guys have all the fun: Inside the world of ESPN.* New York, NY: Back Bay Books.

Molla, R. (2018, June 26). Fortnite is generating more revenue than any other free game ever. *Recode.* Retrieved on March 24, 2020 at: https://www.recode.net/2018/6/26/17502072/fortnite-revenue-game-growth-318-million.

Moore, G. E. (1965). Cramming more components onto integrated circuits. *Electronics, 38*(8). Retrieved on March 24, 2020 at: https://drive.google.com/file/d/0By83v5TWkGjvQkpBcXJKT1I1TTA/view.

Parsons, P. (2003). The evolution of the cable-satellite distribution system. *Journal of Broadcasting & Electronic Media, 47*(1), 1–16.

Pennycock, G., & Rand, D. G. (2019). Lazy, not biased: Susceptibility to partisan fake news is better explained by lack of reasoning than by motivated reasoning. *Cognition, 188*(7), 39–50.

Peyton, J. (2019). What's the average bounce rate for a website? *RocketFuel.* Retrieved on March 24, 2020 at: https://www.gorocketfuel.com/the-rocket-blog/whats-the-average-bounce-rate-in-google-analytics/.

Rabin, R. C. (2018, May 29). Put a ring on it?: Millennial couples are in no hurry. *New York Times.* Retrieved on March 24, 2020 at: https://www.nytimes.com/2018/05/29/well/mind/millennials-love-marriage-sex-relationships-dating.html.

Reutskaja, E., Lindner, A., Nagel, R., Andersen, R. A., & Camerer, C. F. (2018). Choice overload reduces neural signatures of choice set value in dorsal striatum and anterior cingulate cortex. *Nature Human Behaviour, 2*(12), 925–935.

Rodriguez, V. (2018, Dec. 4). How many people play *Fortnite?* Retrieved on March 24, 2020 at: https://www.dbltap.com/posts/6239052-how-many-people-play-fortnite.

Schwartz, B. (2004). *The paradox of choice: Why more is less.* New York: Harper.

Sehgal, K. (2018, Jan. 26). Spotify and Apple Music should become record labels so musicians can make a fair living. *CNBC.* Retrieved on March 24, 2020 at: https://www.cnbc.com/2018/01/26/how-spotify-apple-music-can-pay-musicians-more-commentary.html.

Smirke, R. (2019, June 20). Costly, unethical, improper: Record industry rallies against manipulation of music streams. *Billboard.* Retrieved on March 24, 2020 at: https://www.billboard.com/articles/business/8516841/industry-coalition-streaming-manipulation-code-conduct.

Statista (2019). Average ticket price for music tour concert admission from 2011 to 2018 worldwide in U.S. dollars. Retrieved on March 24, 2020 at: https://www.statista.com/statistics/380106/global-average-music-tour-ticket-price/.

Swanson, A. (2016, Jan. 5). What your new gym doesn't want you to know. *The Washington Post.* Retrieved on March 24, 2020 at: https://www.washingtonpost.com/news/wonk/wp/2016/01/05/what-your-new-gym-doesnt-want-you-to-know/.

"The 2017 Mobile App Report" (2017). *ComScore*. Retrieved on March 24, 2020 at: https://www.comscore.com/Insights/Presentations-and-Whitepapers/2017/The-2017-US-Mobile-App-Report.

Toff, B. & Nielsen, R. K. (2018). 'I just Google it': Folk theories of distributed discovery. *Journal of Communication, 68*(3), 636–657.

Watson, A. (2019, Aug. 13). Number of magazines in the United States from 2002–2018. *Statista*. Retrieved on March 24, 2020 at: https://www.statista.com/statistics/238589/number-of-magazines-in-the-united-states/

The Illusion of Modern Mass Media: False Cultural Barometers and Why Nothing Truly 'Breaks the Internet'

On June 27, 2019, a viral Internet moment was born. Dubbed "Storm Area 51: They Can't Stop All of Us", Matty Roberts had created a nice Facebook web chuckle by urging people to arrive at the location at the same date and time (3 a.m. on September 20, 2019) to find answers and, as one poster promised "to break out our alien homies." It was clearly based in a joke; Roberts had argued that "we can run faster than their bullets. Let's see them aliens." Nevertheless, over two million people said they were going; over 1.5 million more said they were "interested" (Allyn, 2019). Suddenly, this fake event seemed quite real as event spaces were secured, t-shirts and other apparel for "Alienstock" were created, and the American military prepared a response that included an additional 150 officers and 300 paramedics that could counter the potential onslaught. Roberts, the creator of the event, admitted that what started as a joke could become a "possible humanitarian disaster" (Nevett, 2019, para. 5).

Then the fateful day came. For the most part, nothing happened. The 3.5 million people "going" or "interested" had dwindled to 150 people who arrived. Only one person actually crossed the boundary, who was immediately apprehended; the most prevalent crime that was charged was for public urination (Zialcita, 2019). Many lessons could be exacted from the "Storm Area 51" case, but one of the largest was this: just because something appears viral on the Internet does not mean behaviors will change beyond a click and a laugh. Virality no longer meant mass impact. Media interest no longer equated to any imprint upon behavior.

The metrics for virality and audience have changed and, along with them, our perspective in the measurement of their impact is potentially lost. Tolentino (2019) argues that the "possibly most destructive distortion of the internet is its distortion of scale" (p. 29). Storm Area 51 is a prime example of virality that nevertheless fails to materialize. To understand faulty audience metrics, consider the example of the debate-oriented sports talk show.

At the turn of the century, sports talk shows ascended to the forefront of ESPN's programming strategy. *Pardon the Interruption*, featuring veteran sports journalists Tony Kornheiser and Michael Wilbon, debuted to solid ratings in 2001, with *Around the Horn*, with a rotating cast of talking heads, followed the next year. The shows were cheap to produce and were instantly (and continue to be) strong profit-generators for the company.

In 2004, Fox Sports Net launched its challenge to ESPN's talk show supremacy. *I, Max*, featuring lead journalist Max Kellerman with supporting talent Michael Holley, followed similar "discuss the day in 30 minutes" design—albeit with a bit more attitude. Its problem, quite simply, was that nobody watched. In fact, on several occasions, viewership dipped below 50,000 people, resulting in a rounded Nielsen rating of 0.0. Other sports talk shows had similar troubles; CNBC had *McEnroe*, featuring tennis star John McEnroe, which achieved similar rounding distinctions, once scoring a 0.0 while ranking 833rd out of 834 Nielsen rated-cable shows, topping only the Food Network special, *How to Boil Water* (Paulsen, 2009). Such shows were considered, quite simply, to have no audience and, hence, no impact.

Fifteen years later, people tend to concede the television audience is less concentrated (Tice, 2018), yet the argument that it has been placed by the force of Internet influence is often similarly dubious. Those small television audiences of I, Max and McEnroe are gigantic when compared to what it takes to "trend" on a platform like Twitter. Yet, somewhat inexplicably, "trending" is paired with "virality" and "virality" is paired with "influence" (see Kerpen, Greenbaum, & Berk, 2019).

Neyland (2018) explored what it takes to trend on Twitter in late 2018, showing that Twitter has 1.9 million tweets rendered on a typical day, with 631,737 unique tweeters engaged in that process (roughly three per person). Because of time zones, differential levels of Twitter penetration, and sleep patterns, the time of day matters in regard to what it takes for a topic to trend. Still, regardless of the metrics, the number of tweets is truly meager. Using the basic formula of number of people tweeting at any one time about the same topic, Neyland (2018) offers the typical daily standards to have a topic officially "trend" on Twitter:

- Between 12 a.m. to 6 a.m.: approximately 1,200 tweets and about 500 users
- Between 6 a.m. to 12 p.m.: 1,700 tweets and about 733 users
- Between 12 p.m. to 6 p.m.: 1,500 tweets and about 812 users
- Between 6 p.m. to 12 a.m.: 1,900 tweets and about 922 users

All of a sudden, speaking in terms of tens of thousands (as we did for the low-rated television shows) still dwarfs the metrics for trending status. Of course, social media experts would tout impressions (number of people who viewed the tweet) as the most useful metric and they would be correct. However, with the average account having 707 Twitter followers (Smith, 2019) and the average number of people witnessing the tweet at roughly 5% with roughly 1% actually *engaging* with it in an overt manner (Sullivan, 2014), the influence of the majority of trending topics is negligible at best. And yet, somehow, when Twitter topics trend, they are often described setting the Internet "on fire" or even "breaking the Internet"! Granted, some topic reaches truly viral distinction, but the truth is that these cases are few when compared to the less influential second category. Internet power still fails to match legacy media, which is diminishing in its own rite. As Wolff (2015) once explained in the prophetic book *Television is the New Television*, "the closer the new media future gets, the further the victory appears" (p. 1).

This chapter will focus on the myth of virality; it will explore the lack of influence attached to the majority of influential metrics we tend to use. Using examples ranging from the purchase of fake followers to the surprising popularity of Burger King in Pakistan will be employed to show that when it comes to media influence, rarely is there a center—even when we purport there to be one.

"Bowling Alone" Denial

At the turn of the 21st Century, Robert D. Putnam (2000) offered a glimpse of our future by examining our recent past. Using a half million interviews since the mid-1970s, Putnam made the case for communal fragmentation. The number of people joining civic organizations, signing local petitions, or forming neighborhood book clubs was diminishing. As evidenced in the previous chapter, Putnam was chronicling the early age of customization, as people sought to do things in their own ways and in their own manners. Even bowling, Putnam (2000) said, was now more likely to happen alone than in weekly bowling leagues. His influential book, *Bowling Alone: The Collapse and Revival of the American Community*, focused on what Putnam viewed as social capital decay. Others certainly disputed the degree and presence of such decay, arguing that people were clustering in other forms, or as Lehman (1996) contended "kicking in groups," yet it was clear a chord had been struck. Putnam focuses more on community functions than the media tastes we focus on within this book, but nevertheless painted a picture of people who opted for solitary activities that were on their own terms rather than communal activities that must be organized and compromised. And people were doing this all while lamenting that groups do not bond and support each other the way they had in generations past.

The media customization that followed (and which was explained in Chapter 4), cemented these trends. Watercooler shows fell in number; a common touchpoint like Walter Cronkite is nary to be found. Humans feel alone and that feeling is … unsettling. When no one else *does* what you do, you feel like an outcast; you presume no one else *feels* like you do, either, and the stigma grows. The gaps between urban and rural communities become magnified (Saler, 2018) as the ability to find people like your customized self is harder when the populations get smaller, making access to someone acceptable for dating or even socializing difficult in smaller communities.

The isolation can be debilitating. During her failed bid for the 2020 Democratic Presidential nomination, Senator Kamala Harris proposed mental health legislation around "mental health deserts" in rural areas (Arter, 2019), an increasingly serious problem in America. Even worse than struggling with one's mental health, someone living in a rural community with no access to a therapist or psychologist receives a chilling message: there are not enough people like me to warrant a single mental health resource in my community.

We feel alone, customized in our own worlds where it is difficult to find a match of interests where those potential interests have shifted from a handful of types to thousands of unique tastes. The very natural result? One must manufacture commonalities to avoid feeling isolated. Splinters of people can nevertheless be construed as masses. Before the Internet and niche media elements expanded, spiral of silence theory (Noelle-Neumann, 1977) posited that people presumed to be in the minority on an opinion, activity, or interaction, would be more likely to stay quiet to conform to the majority. However, the unintended consequence of the expansion of our digital worlds is that one could find a virtual community for anything. We can now see masses when they are not there. Whether finding others wishing to obsess over a C-list movie star or seeking thousands of people willing to enforce your anorexia as a lifestyle choice (dubbed "pro-ana", Evans, 2017), one can think their community is much larger than it is. Spiral of silence is still in full effect, yet can now be negated by the ability and desire to perceive oneself to be a part of a majority. Masses can be found for virtually any position and a new theory of minority amplification is born. As therapist Travis Stewart tells Evans

(2017), these pockets of sameness can be problematic because "everybody wants to be a part of a community. But they're in a community where they aren't being challenged" (para. 15).

Thus, we move the goal posts on what constitutes mass media influence. Sometimes, as we will show later in this chapter, those metrics can entirely be a mirage. We do it because there is a desire to be able to still say "this is what America does", even if they don't do much of the same things anymore. The Methodist church used to define a "regular" church-goer as someone who attended multiple times each month; now, that definition is applied to anyone attending at least once every six weeks. Television programs report viewership as anyone who "sampled" the content, which is often unpacked as watching a single minute of content ("Unique TV Viewers", n.d.); forget to change the channel after your favorite show is over, and you may now be a "viewer" of a program you can't even name.

As the last chapter showed, our news became customized for our own tastes—which is somewhat problematic—but then, as this chapter endeavors to highlight, we presumed the customized news we were receiving was actually reaching and speaking to a mass audience—which is both wrong and very problematic.

Fake Virality and the Rise of the "Click Farm"

The irregularities began to reveal themselves in 2014. Peculiar trends were uncovered on many social media sites: many of the most popular celebrities and webpages also had one city that was the epicenter of their popularity (Durden, 2014). That city was Dhaka, Bangladesh, boasting a not-insignificant population of roughly 9 million residents. Still, the trends were odd. Dhaka was the most popular location for Facebook likes for everything from Argentinian soccer star Lionel Messi to Google's Facebook page. Dig deeper and results continued to be irregular. The US State Department was most popular ... in Cairo; Burger King's was most popular ... in Karachi, Pakistan (Mendoza, 2014). Celebrities were not immune; singer Katy Perry's popularity surged in these far-away lands, as did Oprah Winfrey and Donald Trump ("Social Media Daily", 2019). What in the world was going on?

The world of "click farms" is the answer. Because "if you make things for the internet, your career sinks or floats on an ocean of clicks. That's true in journalism, on YouTube, and for app creators" (Letzter, 2016, para. 4). While many click farms are now automated and operated via computers/robots, it is still quite common for click farms to thrive using low-cost human labor. Defined by Carr (2018, para. 10) as "an undercover operation in which individuals fraudulently interact with a website to artificially boost the status of a client's website, product or service", click farms operate as a seedy underbelly of modern media influence. Sometimes this is used to enhance perceived credibility on social media; most reason, for instance, that when determining which cleaning company to hire, wouldn't the one with 8,000 likes be the better choice than the one with 57 likes? Sometimes click farms thrive because of the low cost of labor; if a company is willing to pay X for every 10,000 clicks on an advertisement, there is an opportunity to make money from "fake" clicks in nations where they can deliver 10,000 clicks for a fraction of X. Noe (2018) reported on the degrees of the schemes, including a Thai operation that was uncovered in 2017. In this single farm, 476 cellphones and a rotation of 347,200 SIM cards were used to substantially elevate perceived social media influence ("Thailand finds click farm with 347,000 SIM cards", 2017). Some click farms are even larger, with a rotation of 10,000 cellphones creating the faux virality (Noe, 2018).

Utilizing click farms is not without risk, whether that occurs through bad public relations or immediate drop in stock value when discovered to be employing one. However, click farms remain because the short-term risk is seen as negligible to the potential rewards. Those 2014 findings discussed earlier in this section resulted in Oprah losing 11 million followers in a 2014 purge ("Social Media Daily", 2019); Trump lost 15 million in the same process in 2017 (Bort, 2017)—and yet most failed notice or care about the severe adjustments. Meanwhile, the ability to create a false surge in popularity can, indeed, work. Relatively obscure comedy writer Joe Mande attempted to reveal this insider joke to many, boasting 1.01 million Twitter followers and then posting: "twitter is trash, facebook's the devil, i bought a million followers for like $400 none of this shit matters antarctica is melting." He later explained his "meta-joke", contending that:

> The simplest way to tell who's winning the Twitter game is by counting followers. The biggest celebrity accounts—Justin Bieber, Lady Gaga—seem to have millions of followers. But in 2012 I learned that only a portion of those are real humans; some are 'bots,' artificially created to boost an account's popularity. Immediately, I knew that I had found my calling. (Mande, 2016, para. 3)

As a comedian often says: *it's funny because it's true.* But Mande's stock rose since then, finding more fame and interest after this faux-viral stunt nevertheless went viral. The same is true for most of the recipients of fake likes and followers. By the time the click farm surge was removed, each had swelled in popularity with real people; they became products of a self-fulfilling prophecy: people *think* I'm popular, therefore I am.

If Mande was the acknowledgment of how "fake" followers can result in real fame, there is the even more convoluted case of one of the early settlers in this realm: musician Rebecca Black and her 2011 "hit" song "Friday." In late 2010, Black's mother did what many parents do for their aspiring musician children: she paid a company (in this case, Ark Music) money for a low-budget video (in this case, $4,000) and failed to receive much bang for her buck (roughly 1,000 YouTube views in its first month of release). Then, something happened. In early March 2011, Michael J. Nelson, a comedian with 19,000 (presumably mostly real) followers posted Black's video as the answer to the question: "what's the worst video ever made?" Comedy Central comedy show *Tosh.0* showed the clip of the video—and suddenly the video was a thing (Wasserman, 2011). A legitimate thing, at least according to modern metrics. It was a strange phenomenon; by mid-March, "Friday" was on the Billboard Hot 100, despite being played just 12 times (Ehrlich, 2011). The songs virality was tied entirely to a video that, by the end of the month, surpassed Justin Bieber's video for "Baby" as the most disliked music video ever, with more than 1.2 million "thumbs down" (Skarda, 2011). The sensation of the popularity of a video few liked (it now has 3.4 million dislikes at the time of this writing) led to suspicion that the promotion of the video was actually a guerilla marketing stunt "for an upcoming Universal Studios family movie, *The Music Factory*, featuring a fictional character named Rebecca Black played by an actress named Jessica Jones" (Friedman, 2011, para. 2). This turned out to be untrue and left people wondering why a video so chronically bad could continue to gather global support.

The skepticism to which we now must address all metrics of virality is palpable: some things that seem popular (like key social media accounts) are not as popular as they seem; things that seem holistically unpopular (like the video "Friday") is actually meeting metrics that qualify it as, in fact, popular or at least viral/noteworthy. There is little wonder to why Friedman (2011) concludes that "nothing is real on the internet", which is only magnified with the tricks of the trade used today.

Further complicating matters is the (false) presumed democracy of an Internet search. Click farms and other measures of virality thrive when they can predict and understand how to move elements to the fore. When it comes to searches, Google corners the market, with over 90% of all searches taking place on the platform ("Search Engine Market Share Worldwide", 2019). As you develop a theme in this chapter, those searches can be gamed, too. Companies such as Online Reputation Repair and NetReputation exist to move things up or down a Google search listing. This is done in a variety of ways, yet the most prominent appears to be to create desirable content that can subsume the undesirable content and move it down the ranked list of options. This is effective because of human trust in Google rankings as well as laziness in not wishing to search deeply through multiple pages of results. The first result in a Google search gets a click-through rate of roughly 30%, while the last search item on page one has a click-through rate of just 2% (Chaffey, 2018). Bury undesirable content to a second or third page of results, and the information begins to cease existing, with click-through rates well below 1%.

The ability to fix one's reputation online can be a liberating premise—particularly if one's reputation is being smeared through false or later clarified information (say, report of an indictment that proved baseless and was dismissed). Ronson (2015) examined people whose indiscretions and social violations went viral in his book *So You've Been Publicly Shamed*. One chapter focuses exclusively on the liberation that can be found through hiring someone to scrub your personal search history to create a brand new you. However, these manufactured sites (often of benign hobbies such as cat videos or stamp collecting) must still be clicked on en masse—creating the same fake virality as before. You might feel liberated, but the person trying to find out more about you is now perpetually flummoxed by the results generated when searching for you. The common theme again becomes: we trust the system (in this case, Google searches) only to realize the system is frequently gaming us.

Actual Virality and the Rise of "Deepfakes"

Thus far, this chapter has focused on what seems viral and yet isn't, what rises to the fore of Google searches and trending charts yet, for a confluence of reasons, has done so under false societal pretenses. However, the inverse of these phenomena is also quite intriguing: then something actually meets genuine metrics for virality, yet the artifact itself is dubious, artificial or fake.

To be clear, this is not in reference to the bland politician who moves to the top of the polls with promises of a "new day," "fresh start," or other universal platitudes. It is also not in reference to the highly liquid book that gathers throngs of readers yet has no edifying value. It is not even about the pop star whose lyrics about love are repeated 20 times in a single song with a catchy bassline. Instead, this form of fake/artificial virality arises via stories, people, images, and videos that are manufactured; they are events and moments that did not even occur. In the fall of mass communication, anything garnering virality is considered special … even if it's not real.

In this prism, fake news functions differently from what we have discussed earlier in this book, which is spun, tilted, or customized news. Nonetheless, this fake news becomes a cultural touchpoint. Take the 2016 over-the-top story that circulated during the election indicating that Democratic nominee for the

Presidency Hillary Clinton was overseeing a child sex ring through a Washington, D.C. pizza parlor, Comet Ping Pong. While the story was so ridiculous at its core, it was intriguing enough to reverberate. Fox News picked up the story and outlets like the *New York Times* and *Washington Post* decided to respond (Aisch, Huang, & Kang, 2016; Farhi, 2017). Once a man was arrested for carrying a rifle to Comet Ping Pong in response to the hoax that was very much real to him, the story assumed legitimate newsworthiness (Mitchell & Nasaw, 2016). Even then, a Public Policy Polling report showed that 14% of Trump supporters thought the story was real and another 32% were unsure (Jensen, 2016). Fake news proliferated from there; at the time of this writing, #Pizzagate had its own Wikipedia page just to debunk the rumor; a Google search for "Hillary Clinton pizza child sex ring" returns 2.54 million results. A ludicrous story was now a meme; it was worthy of mentioning in Year-End Reviews, disturbingly folding into history.

Such fake news stories were mostly dubbed urban legends before, whether involving the belief that the Great Wall of China can be viewed from outer space (NASA indicates it cannot; "China's Wall Less Great in View from Space", 2005) or Marie Antoinette's famous "let them eat cake" quote (which no record ever has verified). There are enough weird stories that have truth to them (yes, there once was cocaine in Coca-Cola; Lewis, 2012) to make one think that perhaps #Pizzagate is one of those odd but true tales. Add virality, spin, and what you get is a concoction of mainstream influence that sometimes obviates truth from straight-forward stories. Dagnall and Drinkwater (2017) show that urban legends are now "more powerful than ever" (para. 1) because "stories spread so quickly that often it is a case of limiting the spread of fake stories rather than eliminating them" (para. 18). #Pizzagate becomes a story because so many outlets must report on what a non-story it should be. Thus, fake news proliferates and falsehoods endure. When cellphones were first mainstreamed, stories proliferated that linked their usage near gas pumps to spontaneous combustion or other explosions (Mikkelson, 2001); decades later, the myth still is part of some human habits.

People metaphorically throw up their hands in defeat when trying to decipher truth from fiction. False stories piggyback upon real stories; real stories emerge in an attempt to debunk false stories. Reporting is argued as "fake news" (O'Connor & Weatherall, 2018), and misinformation spreads. Even books about fake news, such as Mark Dice's (2017) *The True Story of Fake News: How Mainstream Media Manipulates Millions*, has people on both sides arguing that the reviews for the book (both positive and negative) were manufactured/faked in their own rite for personal reasons.

The result is that people often insist on photos or videos to verify what they can trust. For instance, football player Ray Rice was charged with assault against his fiancé in March 2014; the NFL levied a two-game penalty. When a video of the incident emerged in September 2014, that penalty became an indefinite suspension. Rice would not play a down of professional football again. Many lessons could be taken from the incident (see Richards, Wilson, Boyle, & Mower, 2017), but amongst the most primary: video matters.

Thus, it becomes even more discouraging in our delve into the world of fake virality that "deepfakes" are increasingly utilized and effective. As Talbot (2019) explains, "a deepfake is when an AI algorithm—a neural network—generates [something] that never happened by either swapping one face for another or by allowing someone's motions and voice to be mapped onto another person" (para. 3). We tolerate other forms of fakery—the posthumous Whitney Houston hologram tour, the Dirt Devil ad with a still dancing and very-much-alive Fred Astaire—as the harm seems negligible. However, Metz (2019) shows how fake photos can be utilized to create false online personas, which could then be used for a variety of commercial purposes. Yes, fake virality can result from fake photos posting comments, likes, and other metrics to entities and institutions that society counts on being quite real.

It's not just photos. Donovan (2018) argues that deepfake videos are now "scary good" (para. 1) to the point that there are AI-manipulation systems that can even make someone like Presidents Obama or Trump speak the exact words you say with the exact mannerisms you opt to use. "You laugh or raise an eyebrow," Donovan reports, "and Obama does, too" (para. 15). *The Weekly Standard* dubs such deepfakes a "national security risk" (Lifhits, 2018, para. 16) while *The Wall Street Journal* laments the "destabilizing potential of sophisticated video fakery" Schellmann, 2018, para. 1). In contrast to the artificially produced virality of the click-farm, deepfakes can create real virality in the most seamlessly manufactured way possible. From a faked video of a world leader declaring war to a falsified sex tape used to blackmail, the scope and ramifications of deepfakes are quite extensive. Consider that a video could be produced framing a person for murder is horrifying; the thought that a "deepfake" defense could be used in a trial to release a guilty criminal is also staggeringly real. With deepfakes, we now live in a world where a hoax like #Pizzagate could be revived, with a falsified video of Hillary Clinton confessing to the crime.

The Fall of Cultural Barometers and the Rise of Media Influencers

At this point, one could logically conclude determining mass media influence is all for naught. People and content that seems viral is less so in actuality; things that reach virality are often malicious or deceptive at their core. However, the reason we continue to search for metrics is that we cognitively *need* cultural barometers. These bellwethers are the content of common examples for teachers to use; they are touchpoints in which comedians form their jokes; they are the basis for metaphors writers use to explain the state of the human condition. We need these measures for the same reason that we have top 10 lists and best-seller designations: we want to know what media offerings (and the people within them) are worthy of our time and attention. The Internet Movie Database (IMDB) lists over 1,000 films that are now theatrically released each year; Oscar nominees and Blockbuster distinctions help us sort through the clutter. Over 300 hours of video are uploaded each minute ("37 Mind-Blowing YouTube Facts, Figures and Statistics", 2019); we need to know which ones demand our time and attention. Even if seeking a diversion for a funny cat video, we want to know: which one? Being able to rank and prioritize a vast array of elements is the entire mindset that elevated Buzzfeed, among many other similar competitors.

Cultural barometers become the de facto way in which we move within a flooded media landscape. The catch is that in decades past, media was the mechanism for determining what issues are relevant to a given time period; high ratings for a television program like *Will & Grace* could be viewed as a tipping point for being more inclusive of LGBTQ+ communities, while the rise of Fox News Channel was a harbinger of the previously unquenched thirst for partisan news options. Now, the media platforms themselves are now are the trends in question. A magazine cover used to be an encapsulation of societal trends (such as when *TIME* named "You" as the Person of the Year in 2006 as endemic of the inevitable rise of user-generated media); now that magazine becomes the object of such trends (as people could ask whether weekly magazines are relevant anymore).

Thus, to move the needle, brands merge with culture. By doing so, we "tailor … media consumption to fit … specific interests and needs, shutting out everything they feel is annoying or irrelevant to them" (Thambert, 2019, para. 10) and the options we embrace are those that resonate with values and beliefs. Put simply, when one can customize the culture, one can determine what brand one presumes to be viral in their own world. As Grossman (2018) explains:

> The way brands connect with consumers has changed drastically over the years. It used to be that companies would develop their brand positionings largely through introspection—by identifying what they saw as the defining attributes and benefits of their brand, then pushing that version on to the market. They operated as though they were in complete control. Now, the idea of building brands in such an insular manner feels archaic. Today, brands need to look more actively and purposefully at the culture buzzing around them—in entertainment, in fashion, in news, on social media—and use that awareness to inform how they should best position and integrate themselves

into the world. This is a more powerful form of branding, because by engaging with culture more directly, brands in effect can become a part of that culture, thereby deepening their relevance and connection with customers. And that has never been more prescient or necessary. (para. 1–4)

With social media now as a major component to shaping our personal culture, individuals become people we follow much more than brands. To wit, Apple—one of the most powerful brands in media—has three million followers, while actor Ashton Kutcher boasts six times that amount. In this environment, people become the conduit to our tastes; Apple promoting an Apple Watch on social is dwarfed by the ability of Ashton Kutcher to do so. Hence, the rise of the celebrity influencer.

Celebrity influencers function as the celebrity endorser, yet through highly specialized channels, customized through social media. Joe Gagliese, co-founder of ViralNation, explains that influencers get paid through posts endorsing products because their following seeks parasocial relationships (see Horton & Wohl, 1956) and the desire to emulate or feel close to the person they are following (Leiber, 2018). For them, Gagliese contends, "an endorsement … is just as valuable as working with LeBron. They have incredibly engaged audiences and have an ability to push really big numbers" (Leiber, 2018, para. 20). The amount given to top celebrity influencers are staggering. Reality television star Kylie Jenner receives $1 million per paid Instagram post, while actress/musician Selena Gomez earns $800,000 and soccer standout Cristiano Ronaldo receives $750,000 for every paid post (Mejia, 2018).

Size of audience matters, but even more relevant is the ability to customize and micro-target. Gagliese labels some influencers as micro-influencers (with 10,000–50,000 followers). These people get paid for the type of audiences they have within those smaller swaths of people. "It's like, why pay a celebrity $50 million for a deal when that can be split up among influencers and make real impact?", Gagliese explains (in Leiber, 2018, para. 21). In a mediated version of the in-person TED Talk seminars (which invite a fairly small select list of audience participants and speakers), influencers are used to traverse niche landscapes as companies realize the center of mass media has shrunk considerably.

Of course, such media influencers function differently from (and often in opposition to) the persuasive elements found in formalized digital news media. Bidin (2019, para. 3, 5, 7) articulates three binaries present between the two entities, crystallizing the tensions as:

(a) digital news media's promise of legitimacy vs. influencer's premise of charisma
(b) digital news media's crisis of trustworthiness vs. influencers' burden of relatability
(c) digital news media's accessible legibility vs. influencers' niche reach

THE ILLUSION OF MODERN MASS MEDIA | 115

As Bidin (2019) describes, within the first tension, influencers function in a field of dynamism, which is not directly in contrast to credibility, but does not demand it, either. Digital news media pairs brand with reputation to create legitimacy, tacitly contending "we count because we're established"; influencers argue much of the inverse: "I count because I'm not established." Within the second tension, digital news media still predominantly wishes to convey a feeling of objectivity, whereas influencers convey precisely the opposite, arguing that their relatability leads to their biased choices of one option over another. In other words, where digital news seeks to be informative, influencers only inform to reach the ultimate endgame: to persuade. Within the final tension, digital media companies tether themselves to stay central to the conversation, fragmentation leads to irrelevance or, minimally, less presumed power and centrality. Meanwhile, influencers thrive in insularity. There is a niche quality within their presence that is not repellent and is, conversely, desired. Being untethered to any other entity is the brand in and of itself. In sum, influencers generally accept that they cannot be the center of the media universe, instead aspiring to be the center of their own personalized universe, and to expand that universe accordingly.

So, if there is measurable virality with influencers, one could wonder why these influencers are included in this chapter (about fake virality) and not the previous chapter (about customization). Put simply, it is because we are now finding these media influencers are often built on the same false premises as we have outlined here (Hausman, 2019). Being an influencer became a lifestyle, and a desired one at that. However, as many sought to become influencers, the financial reality was daunting. As Stokel-Walker (2018) summarized, "you can have a million views a month and still not be able to make rent" (para. 1). And, of course, when a system isn't working for someone, there are some who will seek to change—or "game"—the system. Enter the same false metrics as before: fake followers, click farms, and manufactured virality. As documented in the *New York Times*, fake "accounts are counterfeit coins in the booming economy of online influence" (Confessore, Dance, Harris, & Hansen, 2018, para. 6). One company, Devumi, was found in the same story to have over "200,000 customers, including reality television stars, professional athletes, comedians, TED speakers, pastors and models" (para. 11). Everyone was "influencing", yet whom was being influenced was an open question. Websites including sites like Social Envy, fiverr.com, and DIYLikes.com plainly advertised fake followers for fractions of a penny. Influencers still are being paid, but largely because of many companies not yet cognizant to the schemes often being employed. As Hausman (2019) describes, "Social media influencers turn into selling machines. And it's among the top reasons why your marketing campaign may fail" (para. 24).

If there were a case study of what can potentially go wrong when influencers are granted more power than they should exert over products they may not truly endorse, that exemplar would be the calamity that was the 2017 Fyre Festival. Organized by Billy McFarland in collaboration with rapper Ja Rule, the event promised to be a high-end Woodstock in the Bahamas, replete with A-list performers, luxurious accommodations, and VIP packages with six-figure price tags (Wamsley, 2017). The result was an epic disaster: the promised villas became white tents; the music acts failed to appear. The scope of the failure was so magnified that two different documentaries were released in 2019 (one on Netflix, the other on Hulu) so people could witness the schadenfreude of wealthy attendees seeking the hot ticket to an exclusive beach paradise that failed in every manner.

The way Fyre Festival lured people to the event was a promise of the "cultural event of the decade" (Wamsley, 2017, para. 9). In a now-deleted tweet, Ja Rule assured everyone that the Fyre Festival would be "where all the cool kids will be." The organizers' evidence of cool kid interest was a cadre of highly-paid media influencers. Kendall Jenner, Bella Hadid, Emily Ratajkowski, and many others posted (for $125,000 each) appealing and provocative videos on social media promising "transformative weekends" (Burrough, 2017, para. 18). When the truth of the woefully-underfunded festival came to light, these influencers cancelled their appearances, paid to promote Fyre Festival without knowing what it was really about or whether they would actually attend. In the end, a reported $5.3 million was spent on media influencers—all for an event with no real structure or chance to succeed (Singh-Kurtz, 2019).

In the end, it's clear to see that media influencers can work (witness the thousands flying to a doomed festival) while still having structural flaws in the system (people regarded these influencers as trustworthy institutions rather than the autonomous charisma magnets Bidin (2019) articulates in her three primary tensions. Most celebrities weren't ordering these opportunities to influence through their massive social followings. Rather, social media experts, desperate to prove their worth, push a model that can work—but only if what is promoted comes within viable, organized structures. Media influencers can attract people to virtually anything—even something fabricated at its core.

The Desire for Consensus Narratives

The day before Thanksgiving 2019, Netflix released a film that would become an immediate Oscar frontrunner, Martin Scorsese's *The Irishman*. The fact that an awards favorite from a beloved director was available as part of a Netflix subscription attracted 13.2 million viewers in the first five days. Pundits pontificated that such a large swath of viewers staying home to watch a movie resulted in fewer people at the multiplex (CITE), creating a form of *Irishman* effect. However, less reported was the proportion of the 13.2 million viewers who finished the entire movie (just 18%; Shaw, 2019), which meant that 2.37 million viewers was the more adequate claim. Keep in mind that this was a movie that was offered for no additional cost on top of a Netflix subscription, but even if we were to assume that all 2.37 million viewers would have paid for a ticket to the film, the total would have been $21.9 million.

The common thread throughout this chapter is the endeavor to separate mountains from molehills, with the context of this thread being that there are many molehills conspicuously disguised as mountains. The case of *The Irishman* is not a Netflix anomaly; another of its biggest hits, 2018's *Bird Box*, had similar completion numbers while *Breaking Bad* companion film *El Camino* was completed by just 11% of the viewers who started it (Shaw, 2019). The desire for common touchpoints leads us to want to believe there are still many things that "everyone" does. When the 2018 film *Bohemian Rhapsody* surprises all expectations with a $69 million domestic gross its opening weekend, we not only want to express surprise, but complete the narrative: look what everyone did this weekend. The truth is that with a roughly $9.11 per person average ticket price at the time, 7.5 million Americans (2.2% of the population) watched the film. That was better than all other films for the weekend, yet still is niche and non-viral at its opening.

Why do we ascribe influence when the evidence is, at best, uneven? Many reasons could be attached to the bolstering of social media influence, but arguably the largest resides in the fact that journalists constitute less than 1% of any nation's population, yet constitute nearly a quarter (24.6%) of all Twitter user accounts (Morrison, 2015). Guerrero (2018) summarized new proposed guidelines for journalists at the *New York Times*, yet the guidelines focused primarily on avoiding partisan social media posts and on accepting that personal accounts of *NYT* staffers are nonetheless subject to the same standards. Such guidelines neglect to focus on the elements of fake virality outlined in this chapter, whether out of naivety or, more likely, the inability to adequately enact a new plan for quoting posters on social media that offers enough clarity for journalists to follow.

While social media outlets like Facebook work to ensure viable information sharing that includes a sense of moderating of falsification (both of news and of the degree to which that news creates ripple effects), Bell (2018) explains that "the overall effect is that the fake news and the spam sites and the viral sites are meant to be less prominent in the news feed, and higher quality news more so. The problem is we just don't know how that's going to play out, and I don't think Facebook knows either" (para. 24).

Determining the end game for this continually-shifting landscape is obviously a yeoman's task. However, it is the hope that this chapter aided in making you sufficiently paranoid about the notion of virality and the degree to which the metric could aptly and ably be applied. Virality certainly happens in media—and specifically on social platforms. However, the bar is much lower than it should be and not all those that would even clear a higher bar would constitute virality without false metrics. The Internet never breaks—and if it ever did, it may be because of a click farm in a foreign land, offering false clicks and views on media content offerings in which they may not have any interest in the first place.

References

"37 Mind-Blowing YouTube Facts, Figures and Statistics" (2019). *MerchDope*. Retrieved on March 24, 2020 at: https://merchdope.com/youtube-stats/.

Aisch, G., Huang, J., & Kang, C. (2016, Dec. 10). Dissecting the #PizzaGate conspiracy theories. *The New York Times*. Retrieved on March 24, 2020 at: https://www.nytimes.com/interactive/2016/12/10/business/media/pizzagate.html.

Allyn, B. (2019, July 15). More than one million agree to 'storm Area 51', but the Air Force stays stay home. *NPR*. Retrieved on March 24, 2020 at: https://www.npr.org/2019/07/15/741938966/more-than-1-million-people-agree-to-storm-area-51-but-the-air-force-says-stay-ho.

Arter, M. (2019, Feb. 20). Senator Kamala Harris: We have mental health 'deserts' in our country. *CNS News*. Retrieved on March 24, 2020 at: https://www.cnsnews.com/news/article/melanie-arter/sen-kamala-harris-we-have-mental-health-deserts-our-country.

Bell, E. (2018, Apr. 19). Can journalism survive the onslaught of social media. *Unherd*. Retrieved on March 24, 2020 at: https://unherd.com/2018/04/can-journalism-can-survive-onslaught-social-media/.

Bidin, C. (2019, Feb. 5). Three opposing barometers between digital news media and influencers. *Cyborgology*. Retrieved on March 24, 2020 at: https://thesocietypages.org/cyborgology/2019/02/05/three-opposing-barometers-between-the-digital-news-media-and-influencers/.

Bort, R. (2017, May 30). Nearly half of Donald Trump's Twitter followers are fake accounts and bots. *Newsweek*. Retrieved on March 24, 2020 at: https://www.newsweek.com/donald-trump-twitter-followers-fake-617873.

Burrough, B. (2017, June 29). Fyre festival: Anatomy of a millennial marketing fiasco waiting to happen. *Vanity Fair*. Retrieved on March 24, 2020 at: https://www.vanityfair.com/news/2017/06/fyre-festival-billy-mcfarland-millennial-marketing-fiasco.

Carr, S. (2018, June 25). What is a click farm? The quick way to thousands of likes. *PPC Protect*. Retrieved on March 24, 2020 at: https://ppcprotect.com/what-is-a-click-farm/.

Chaffey, D. (2018, July 9). Comparison of Google clickthrough rates by position. *Smart Insights*. Retrieved on March 24, 2020 at: https://www.smartinsights.com/search-engine-optimisation-seo/seo-analytics/comparison- of-google-clickthrough-rates-by-position/.

"China's Wall Less Great in View from Space" (2005, May 9). *NASA Report*. Retrieved on March 24, 2020 at: https://www.nasa.gov/vision/space/workinginspace/great_wall.html.

Confessore, N., Dance, G. J. X., Harris, R., & Hansen, M. (2018, Jan. 27). The follower factory. *New York Times*. Retrieved on March 24, 2020 at: https://www.nytimes.com/interactive/2018/01/27/technology/social-media-bots.html.

Dagnall, N., & Drinkwater, K. (2017, May 15). Why urban legends are more powerful than ever. *The Conversation*. Retrieved on March 24, 2020 at: https://theconversation.com/why-urban-legends-are-more-powerful-than-ever-76718.

Dice, M. (2017). *The true story of fake news: How mainstream media manipulates millions*. Seattle, WA: Resistance Manifesto.

Donovan, J. (2018, Sept. 5). Deepfake videos are getting scary good. How stuff works. Retrieved on March 24, 2020 at: https://electronics.howstuffworks.com/future-tech/deepfake-videos-scary-good.htm.

Durden, T. (2014, Jan. 6). It's a click farm world: 1 million followers cost $600 and the State Department buys 2 million likes. Retrieved on March 24, 2020 at: https://www.zerohedge.com/news/2014-01-06/its-click-farm-world-1-million-followers-cost-600-and-state-department-buys-2-millio.

Ehrlich, B. (2011, Mar. 25). Not *that* fun: Rebecca Black gets played just 12 times on the radio. *Mashable*. Retrieved on March 24, 2020 at: https://mashable.com/2011/03/25/rebecca-black-radio/#KiiJu1F.PsqK.

Evans, R. (2017, Feb. 11). The bizarre world of the pro-anorexia internet community. *Cracked*. Retrieved on March 24, 2020 at: https://www.cracked.com/personal-experiences-2452-a-look-inside-disturbingly-large-pro-anorexia-community.html.

Farhi, P. (2017, May 17). A conspiratorial tale of murder, with Fox News at the center. *The Washington Post*. Retrieved on March 24, 2020 at: https://www.washingtonpost.com/lifestyle/style/a-conspiratorial-tale-of-murder-with-fox-news-at-the-center/2017/05/17/6a4d1f5a-3b14-11e7-a058-ddbb23c75d82_story.html?utm_term=.9929bd261dd6.

Friedman, U. (2011, Apr. 11). Nothing is real on the internet: 'Rebecca Black is fake' story is fake. *The Atlantic*. Retrieved on March 24, 2020 at: https://www.theatlantic. com/entertainment/archive/2011/04/nothing-real-internet-ever-rebecca-black-not-fictional-character/349531/.

Grossman, P. (2018, Aug. 10). How do brands become part of our culture? *Forbes*. Retrieved on March 24, 2020 at: https://www.forbes.com/sites/quora/2018/08/10/how-do-brands-become-part-of-our-culture/#242cf077935d.

Guerrero, R. (2018, Sept. 18). The ethical issues of social media in journalism. *Medium*. Retrieved on March 24, 2020 at: https://medium.com/@ryan.guerrero/the-ethical-issues-of-social-media-in-journalism-430c85ca8fd1.

Hausman, A. (2019, Jan. 17). The rise and fall of the social media influencer. *Marketing Insider Group*. Retrieved on March 24, 2020 at: https://marketinginsidergroup.com/influencer-marketing/the-rise-and-fall-of-the-social-media-influencer/.

Horton, D., & Wohl, R. (1956). Mass communication and parasocial interaction: Observation on intimacy at a distance. *Psychiatry, 19*(3), 215–229.

Jensen, T. (2016, Dec. 9). Trump remains unpopular; voters prefer Obama on SCOTUS pick. *Public Policy Polling*. Retrieved on March 24, 2020 at: https://www.publicpolicypolling.com/polls/trump-remains-unpopular-voters-prefer-obama-on-scotus-pick/.

Kerpen, D., Greenbaum, M., & Berk, R. (2019). *Likeable social media: How to delight your customers, create an irresistible brand, & be generally amazing on all the social networks that matter* (3rd Ed.). New York: McGraw-Hill.

Lehman, N. (1996, April). Kicking in groups. *The Atlantic*. Retrieved on March 24, 2020 at: https://www.theatlantic.com/magazine/archive/1996/04/kicking-in-groups/376562/.

Leiber, C. (2018, Nov. 28). How and why do influencers make so much money?: The head of an influencer agency explains. *Vox*. Retrieved on March 24, 2020 at: https://www.vox.com/the-goods/2018/11/28/18116875/influencer-marketing-social-media-engagement-instagram-youtube.

Letzter, R. (2016, June 27). Yes, the click farms on HBO's 'Silicon Valley' are a real thing and they aren't going away. *Business Insider*. Retrieved on March 24, 2020 at: https://www.businessinsider.com/silicon-valley-are-click-farms-real-2016-6.

Lewis, D. (2012, Feb. 24). What happened to the cocaine in Coca-Cola? *Business Insider*. Retrieved on March 24, 2020 at: https://www.businessinsider.com/what-happened-to-the-cocaine-in-coca-cola-2012-2.

Lifhits, J. (2018, July 20). Deepfakes are coming. And they're dangerous. *The Weekly Standard*. Retrieved on March 24, 2020 at: https://www.weeklystandard.com/jenna-lifhits/deepfake-videos-are-a-national-security-threat.

Mande, J. (2016, Nov. 28). How I learned to game Twitter. *The New Yorker*. Retrieved on March 24, 2020 at: https://www.newyorker.com/magazine/2016/11/28/how-i-learned-to-game-twitter.

Mejia, Z. (2018, July 31). Kylie Jenner reportedly makes $1 million per paid Instagram post here's how much other top influencers get. *CNBC*. Retrieved on March 24, 2020 at: https://www.cnbc.com/2018/07/31/kylie-jenner-makes-1-million-per-paid-instagram-post-hopper-hq-says.html.

Mendoza, M. (2014, Jan. 5). Selling social media clicks becomes big business. *Associated Press*. Retrieved on March 24, 2020 at: https://www.apnews.com/c90f39b90c9d41eca bb60db98c0042ba.

Metz, R. (2019, Feb. 28). These people do not exist. Why websites are churning out fake images of people (and cats). *CNN Business*. Retrieved on March 24, 2020 at: https://amp.cnn.com/cnn/2019/02/28/tech/ai-fake-faces/index.html.

Mikkelson, D. (2001, Apr. 10). Is cell phone use at gas pumps dangerous? *Snopes*. Retrieved on March 24, 2020 at: https://www.snopes.com/fact-check/fuelish-pleasures/.

Mitchell, J., & Nasaw, D. (2016, Dec. 4). Man arrested with gun at Comet Ping Pong, Washington eatery subject of fake news hoax. *The Wall Street Journal*. Retrieved on March 24, 2020 at: https://blogs.wsj.com/washwire/2016/12/04/man-arrested-with-gun-at-comet-ping-pong-washington-eatery-subject-of-fake-news-hoax/.

Morrison, K. (2015, June 1). Report: Journalists make up a quarter of all verified Twitter accounts. *AdWeek*. Retrieved on March 24, 2020 at: https://www.adweek.com/digital/report-journalists-make-up-a-quarter-of-all-verified-twitter-accounts/.

Nevett, J. (2019, Sept. 13). Storm Area 51: The joke that became a possible humanitarian disaster. *BBC News*. Retrieved on March 24, 2020 at: https://www.bbc.com/news/world-us-canada-49667295.

Neyland, K. (2018, Nov. 23). How many tweets does it take to trend? *Jungle Marketing*. Retrieved on March 24, 2020 at: https://jungle.marketing/news/how-many-tweets-does-it-take-to-trend/.

Noe, R. (2018, Dec. 11). Eye-opening photos and video taken inside illegal click farms: phone-y engagement. *Core 77*. Retrieved on March 24, 2020 at: https://www.core77.com/posts/81665/Eye-Opening-Photos-and-Video-Taken-Inside-Illegal-Click-Farms.

Noelle-Neumann, E. (1977). Turbulences in the climate of opinion: Methodological applications of the spiral of silence theory. *Public Opinion Quarterly, 41*(2), 143–158.

O'Connor, C., & Weatherall, J. O. (2018). *The misinformation age: How false beliefs spread*. New Haven, CT: Yale University Press.

Paulsen (2009). Decade in review: 10 worst sports shows. *Sports Media Watch*. Retrieved on March 24, 2020 at: http://www.sportsmediawatch.com/2009/12/decade-in-review-10-worst-sports-shows/.

Putnam, R. D. (2000). *Bowling alone: The collapse and revival of the American community*. New York: Simon & Schuster.

Richards, O., Wilson, C., Boyle, K., & Mower, J. (2017). A knockout to the NFL's reputation?: A case study of the NFL's crisis communications strategies in response to the Ray Rice scandal. *Public Relations Review, 43*(3), 615–623.

Ronson, J. (2015). *So you've been publicly shamed*. New York: Penguin.

Saler, T. (2018, Apr. 20). Tom Saler: The gap between rural and urban America is growing wider. *The Milwaukee Journal Sentinel*. Retrieved on March 24, 2020 at: https://www.jsonline.com/story/money/business/2018/04/20/tom-saler-gap-between-rural-and-urban-america-growing-wider/537750002/.

Schellmann, H. (2018, Oct. 15). Deepfake videos are getting real and that's a problem. *The Wall Street Journal* (Video). Retrieved on March 24, 2020 at: https://www.wsj.com/video/series/moving-upstream/deepfake-videos-are-getting-real-and-that-a-problem/0C3815FB-82C7-4805-B902-31BEB0B4F146.

"Search Engine Market Share Worldwide." (2019, Mar.). *Statcounter*. Retrieved on March 24, 2020 at: http://gs.statcounter.com/search-engine-market-share.

Shaw, L. (2019, Dec. 6). 'The Irishman' is a Netflix hit, even if few make it to the end. *Bloomberg News*. Retrieved on March 24, 2020 at: https://www.bloomberg.com/news/articles/2019-12-06/-the-irishman-is-a-netflix-hit-even-if-few-make-it-to-the-end.

Singh-Kurtz, S. (2019, Apr. 17). Fyre Festival's trustee hopes Netflix and Hulu can pay some of its debts. *Quartz*. Retrieved on March 24, 2020 at: https://qz.com/1598012/fyre-festival-bankruptcy-trustee-seeks-netflix-and-hulu-cash/.

Skarda, E. (2011, Mar. 30). Rebecca Black surpasses Justin Bieber as most disliked on YouTube. *TIME*. Retrieved on March 24, 2020 at: http://newsfeed.time.com/2011/03/30/rebecca-black-passes-justin-bieber-as-most-disliked-on-youtube/.

Smith, K. (2019, Jan. 3). 58 incredible and interesting Twitter stats and statistics. *Brandwatch*. Retrieved on March 24, 2020 at: https://www.brandwatch.com/blog/twitterstats-and-statistics/.

Social Media Daily (2019). Do celebrities buy Instagram followers & does it work out for them? Retrieved on March 24, 2020 at: https://www.socialmediadaily.com/blog/do-celebrities-buy-instagram-followers.

Stokel-Walker, C. (2018, Feb. 27). Success on YouTube still means a life of poverty. *Bloomberg*. Retrieved on March 24, 2020 at: https://www.bloomberg.com/news/articles/2018-02-27/-success-on-youtube-still-means-a-life-of-poverty.

Sullivan, D. (2014, July 11). Just like Facebook, Twitter's new impression stats suggest few followers see what's tweeted. *Marketing Land*. Retrieved on March 24, 2020 at: https://marketingland.com/facebook-twitter-impressions-90878.

Talbot, M. (2019, Feb. 23). Deepfakes explained: How technology is masking reality. *CTV News*. Retrieved on March 24, 2020 at: https://www.ctvnews.ca/sci-tech/deepfakes-explained-how-technology-is-masking-reality-1.4308838.

"Thailand finds click farm with 347,000 SIM cards" (2017, June 13). *Associated Press*. Retrieved on March 24, 2020 at: https://www.presstv.com/DetailFr/2017/06/13/525171/Thailand-Police-SIM-Cards.

Thambert, F. (2019, Jan. 21). Why brands must become part of culture to stay relevant. *Klarna. Knowledge*. Retrieved on March 24, 2020 at: https://www.klarna.com/knowledge/articles/why-brands-must-become-part-of-culture-to-stay-relevant/.

Tice, D. C. (2018). *The genius box: How the 'idiot box' got smart & is changing the television business*. Pennsauken, NJ: BookBaby Publishing.

Tolentino, J. (2019). *Trick mirror: Reflections on self delusion*. New York: Random House.

"Unique TV Viewers" (n.d.). *eventIMPACTS*. Retrieved on March 24, 2020 at: http://www.eventimpacts.com/impact-types/media/content/volume-of-coverage/basic-measures/unique-tv-viewers.

Wamsley, L. (2017, Apr. 28). Paradise lost: Luxury music festival turns out to be half-built scene of chaos. *NPR*. Retrieved on March 24, 2020 at: https://www.npr.org/sections/thetwo-way/2017/04/28/526019457/paradise-lost-luxury-music-festival-turns-out-to-be-half-built-scene-of-chaos.

Wasserman, T. (2011, Mar. 16). How Rebecca Black became a YouTube sensation. *Mashable*. Retrieved on March 24, 2020 at: https://mashable.com/2011/03/16/rebecca-black-youtube/#JDDKcQxH4Sq0.

Wolff, M. (2015). *Television is the new television: The unexpected triumph of old media in the digital age*. New York, NY: Portfolio Publishing.

Zialcita, P. (2019, Sept. 20). Storm Area 51 fails to materialize. *NPR*. Retrieved on March 24, 2020 at: https://www.npr.org/2019/09/20/762897934/storm-area-51-fails-to-materialize.

CHAPTER SIX

"Don't Tell Me; I'm Not Caught Up!": Death of the Watercooler

It has been said that talking about music is like dancing about architecture. The formats of style fail to match. Doing so is difficult—and yet people have attempted to talk about music since the beginning of the mass produced written word. Why? Because when a musical piece of art enters one's atmosphere, it seemingly demands to be acknowledged. The experience urges the listener to share. The remedy to this communicative mismatch becomes readily apparent, as the song is short enough (typically three to four minutes), that it becomes easier to spread word of a song by asking someone to listen to it—or be re-listening to it along with a friend.

Other media formats demand ramifications as well, yet are more easily discussed than music, hence the book club or the Twitter dissection of a noteworthy political convention speech. However, there are still media events that rise above more casual fare. We repeatedly ascribe to the notion that the revolution will be televised, and there is nothing quite like a movie or TV show depicting a moment where everyone is witnessing the same event with fixed eyes on the same moment—the shot of global persons each transfixed by a bar or restaurant screen has become symbolic for the epic mediated moment in which all must care. Personal moments that are key in an individuals' life are important, to be sure, yet the key moments are the ones a society continually revisits. "Where were you when …" is completed in different ways for different generations, whether that sentence is completed with "… Kennedy was shot" for Baby Boomers, "the Miracle on Ice" or "… the Challenger exploded" for Generation X'ers, or "… the Twin Towers fell" for Generation Y'ers.

As audacious as it might seem to compare the fragmentation of various forms of entertainment culture to such hard news, horrific moments in each generations' imprinted past, the reality is that 24/7 news creates so many breaking news stories as to make very few rise to the level of consistent conversation, whether face-to-face or via other online formats. That leaves things that seem frivolous, but are actually about the connective tissue of what is intended to fuse seemingly disparate American experiences into one societal fabric. As Disney CEO Bob Iger told *Time* magazine's Luscombe (2019):

> There's never been a time when art and entertainment are as important as today. I think people are desperate for it, and I think that our place in the world is both important and something that I'm extremely proud of, to be in this business at this company at this point, at this time in the world. I don't look at what we do as frivolous. I don't look at what we do as small. I don't look at what we do as inconsequential. (p. 60)

Thus, this chapter is about what was and yet no longer is within the notion of the cultural watercooler. More specifically, it will focus on the trade-off between the customization discussed in Chapter 4 and the common language inferred throughout the book. Forty years after Todd Gitlin's seminal (1980) tome on mass media, led with the title *The Whole World is Watching*, a succinct post-media fragmentation, post-script response to Gitlin offered in the chapter is that no, the whole world no longer is watching—now what?

Now or Later: The Urgency of Media Liquidity

Imagine, for a moment, that Beyoncé and Jay-Z released a new album and everyone who heard it thought it was groundbreakingly epic … but the only people permitted to hear it for weeks were Grammy voters. Imagine HBO's *Game of Thrones* released its final slate of episodes with viewers finally witnessing the epic series' end game … but the program was only released in tiny segments of Pittsburgh and Phoenix. Imagine that the Super Bowl secured a new contract that would make the National Football League a ton of money … but the game could only be witnessed by those with contracts for AT&T Wireless. All of these scenarios sound far-fetched and, one could argue, apocryphal at their core. They drip with elitism, exclusiveness, or snobbery in a manner that likely could repel those who thought they were interested in these media products. And yet this is not that different from how most prestigious, Academy Award-aspiring films are released in 2020. If the watercooler is dying, the film industry blazed the trail on how to kill it.

Certain films still secure very wide releases—wider than ever before. The five widest releases of all-time came in 2019, even at a time when the number of theatres and stayed generally flat over the past decade (National Association of Theatre Owners, 2019). This could be used to argue that the mass, shared media experience still exists, yet it is even more endemic of the peakedness of the curve; when a single film can command such a large portion of the screens and stay in that location for months, the opportunity for consistent shared experiences drops to a handful of moments—and, even then, one better like comic book movies in order to experience them. Similar trends happen in other fields. In sports media, the mass proliferation of sports channels and options have led to a very concentrated center on flagship offerings; Cooky, Messner, and Musto (2015) found that nearly three-quarters of all ESPN *SportsCenter* programming was of three sports: football, baseball, and men's basketball. When so few things occupy the center, everything else is a niche.

Modern film offerings, then, occupy a bizarre space for the cinephile: one in which people in the large population centers (New York, Los Angeles) can seek out virtually every film upon release while the majority of the geographic imprint of a nation hopes the film might come to town. More often than not, the film is first available to these smaller population centers months later via DVD and streaming platforms, long after any watercooler conversation could have reasonably been advanced. Film trailers claiming that a release "starts everywhere" on a certain date are almost always fibbing. Consuming all of the Oscar-nominated films is a downright chore for many who even are willing to make the task a priority.

Where most films lack watercooler elements comes not from a lack of *desire* to take part; rather, they come from a lack of *ability* to do so. There is a liquidity to modern media that gets ever-smaller as years progress. Imagine an Internet meme that half the nation could not access for months; the desire to discuss could long pass before opportunity for conversation would present itself.

Hence, media becomes about *urgency*. The ability to consume something now—or even early—is a stimulant for the interested party. In 2013, Paramount offered what initially sounded like a ridiculous prospect: a "mega-ticket" in which one would pay $50 to watch the new Brad Pitt-led film, *World War Z*. Offered in five different cities, Included in this purchase would be: a ticket to a RealD 3D screening of the film, customized 3D glasses, access to a DVD or streaming copy of the film when it was released, a limited edition movie poster, and a small popcorn (Deming, 2013). All were potentially appealing to fans eager to see the film, yet the top reason people flocked to purchase this mega-ticket was even simpler: people got to screen the film two days *before* the national release. The *World War Z* mega-ticket was an insider's dream.

Examples such as this illustrate the increased importance the modern media audience places on urgency. When determining what media to consume, urgency is measured in a variety of ways. The first is immediacy, an undercurrent to the decision that tells the consumer what media is appealing and yet will not be in a short length of time. In this ecosystem, reality programs like *The Bachelorette* and award shows like the Emmys or the Oscars take precedent over the scripted. With millions of media choices ranging from a new podcast to the morning newspaper to a viral Snapchat post, people must select what deserves their attention *now*. Hierarchies are formed whether one recognizes them or not; a viral video gets precedent over a new book, as the discussion of the former is measured in minutes whereas for the latter (if the book is worthwhile), conversations of it would be measured in years. A conservative might consider an evening episode of *Tucker Carlson Tonight* a top priority; that same episode moves far to the back of the media rankings just one day later.

A second mechanism for determining urgency is the stakes we perceive to be involved. The mantra of previous generations likely was questioning whether anything worthwhile was on television or at the movie theater at a given time; that question has now been replaced by what deserves priority in a truly flooded media environment. No one asks if there's anything "new" on YouTube and no one scours the Internet to find they have read everything they were interested in. When finite space (newspaper pages; programming channels) are replaced by infinite band-width (300 hours of YouTube content added each minute; 5,579 movie/television titles in the Netflix library; Smith, 2019), one would need to be comatose to not find anything appealing to consume.

Thus, one must make choices based on the urgency of the content being offered. A presidential debate likely could take precedence over a new article in *Salon*. A basketball playoff game could trump an episode of *The Good Place*. When a battle for "most-subscribed" YouTube account gets tight—as it did between Pew Die Pie and T-Series in 2019—people flock to bear witness with an urgency that the new Elizabeth Gilbert novel cannot muster. The battle for one's attention becomes nearly comical, with "breaking news" being promised on cable news networks with such regularity that some consider it neither breaking nor news. In sum, priorities are not necessarily formed through any notion of preferring media object A over media object B; rather, both A and B (and C-Z) are assessed through the lens of urgency, asking oneself: "what media would provide gratification now, but not necessarily a day or week from now?"

Finally, we determine urgency based on what is potentially a watercooler discussion, which we still crave. Perhaps someone loves a niche program on a nascent streaming network—but the chances of that becoming something that is organically discussed at lunch or with colleagues is relatively nil. Thus, watching this content is tabled while one consumes a presidential debate or new Taylor Swift video, each of which may very well be something more likely to be part of discussions or Facebook feeds the next day. Every day that passes makes a watercooler conversation less likely to happen. Every less watercooler moment is one less thread in the shared societal conversation.

Missing Mavens: A Link Gone in Trending Matrices

Malcolm Gladwell's (2002) popular juggernaut of a book, *The Tipping Point*, argued that three key types of individuals are essential to starting trends and epidemics within culture: connectors (who know many individuals and bridge networks in substantial manners), mavens (who enjoy the act/art of determining what new advents are worth endorsing to others), and salesmen, (who become the point people to convince others that a certain trend/change in culture is worth embracing).

The changes described in this book have very clearly accelerated two of these three types of people. For instance, connectors have always been important, as shown in the famous "six degrees of separation" study from Milgram (1967), who showed virtually any American could be linked by the right combination of six individual connections. Now, thanks to the advent of the Internet and social media in particular, that number has shrunk dramatically from six degrees to two (Christley, 2017). Yes, there is likely a person who can mostly likely connect you to Barack Obama or LeBron James; the key is finding that singular connector. Connectors' jobs are infinitely easier than before. LinkedIn facilitates career connections. Facebook facilitates conversations between one's third grade elementary school teacher and your next-door neighbor. A whopping 85% of all jobs are now attained, at least to some demonstrable degree, via networking (Adler, 2016). Connectors' jobs are now easier than ever before.

Salesmen also, similarly, have a much easier job in the age of ubiquitous media. Salesmen have the ability to launch webpages, social media accounts, YouTube channels and the like to build one's brand. One can, from their own proverbial basement, induce/influence millions of others to adopt or reject certain products, content, or behaviors if that person possesses those unique qualities that constitute a true social salesman. Even a seven-year old, host of "Ryan's Toy Reviews," can garner 18 million subscribers and monetize his operation to over $22 million each year if one is sufficiently virally persuasive (Maven, 2019). Salesmen again have it easier in the modern media not just because of the interconnectivity, but also because of the ability for any person to (relatively effortlessly and cost-effectively) become a media producer.

Meanwhile, mavens represent the weak link in this chain described by Gladwell. Media mavens' jobs are now harder than ever before. *Infinitely* harder. In the 1980s, roughly 120 films were released each year; that number has now sextupled to nearly 750 films. Television now has nearly 500 different scripted series produced each year, with streaming increasing its overall number of scripted entries by 385% in the five years from 2014–2018 (Hibbard, 2018). The number of news-based websites is so massive that when one ranks the top 100, as *Feedspot* did in 2019, message boards are filled with people suggesting viable options that were omitted.

There is so much to consume that there is hardly any time left to interact about that media or other non-media related things. Michos (2019) reports of "sitting disease" (para. 1), partly resulting from an all-time low of American jobs that are active/movement-related (20%) and partly because of ties to screen-related content. Americans now sit more than any time in recorded history (Fisher, 2019) at least in part due to content that is as much overwhelming as it is appealing.

Thus, the maven's life is now rendered virtually impossible, careening from one week's top media offering to another, all while trying to avoid spoilers or provide references in which some likely would not "get." The vast array of options leads to the presumed need for the media influencer articulated in Chapter 5: there needs to be some gateway in which to navigate the clutter.

Media in Isolation: Small Screens, Small Audiences

As habits of a culture change, so do the psychological needs of the people within a society. Many of our new media habits have become solitary for a variety of reasons. For instance, binge-watching begets single-person viewing (Rubenking, Bracken, Sandoval, & Rister, 2018) as millions of options and speeds of consumption make it difficult for even two people to agree on the type and pace of that content. A study from UK-based OfCom (2017) finds that 90% of viewers now regularly do so alone. Many other media advents make the experience more isolated; a smartphone screen is hard to share with more than one set of eyes, leading to the awkward yet prevalent sight of a group of six teenagers silently sitting together, each staring at text streams on their phones. Even news—in an age in which it comes in many shapes, volumes, and flavors—is difficult to agree upon even among like-minded people, so that, too, is increasingly consumed individually.

All of this leads to what Schulze (2018) dubs the "new great public epidemic": loneliness, a problem which Murthy (2017) finds is as detrimental as smoking 15 cigarettes per day. This isolation is particularly pronounced in younger people, with a quarter of millennials now indicating that they do not have a single friend, leading Lanigan (2019) to dub them the "loneliest generation" (para. 1). Perhaps it is a stretch to state media has a primary role in this isolation, but it is a fairly convincing argument to claim all of these forms of media play some substantial function. Consider the following two graphs that represent the most-discussed topics on Facebook and Instagram for one representative month, April 2018 (as offered from Facebook IQ, 2018).

Looking at each chart, it does not take long to see how people are using media to discuss media. While the list also include everything from holidays to many types of food and drink, the majority of the items in each list are elements that are inherently mediated, ranging from awards shows (Daytime Emmys, Academy of Country Music Awards) to singers (Post Malone, Cardi B) to sports figures (Conor McGregor, Dallas Cowboys). Even the news items were less about policy and more about media figures, including FOX News' Sean Hannity and the speaker for the televised (and later streamed) White House Correspondents' Dinner, Michelle Wolf. Even Facebook's six main categories (brands and products, entertainment, food and drink, holidays and events, people and culture, and sports) feature a range of topics that are about media. Lest one think that this is simply a social media platform predisposed to media topics, note that the main topics are not all that different than the earlier interpersonal findings of Bischoping (1993), identifying five main categories of conversation: leisure activity, people and relationships, work and money, issues, and appearances.

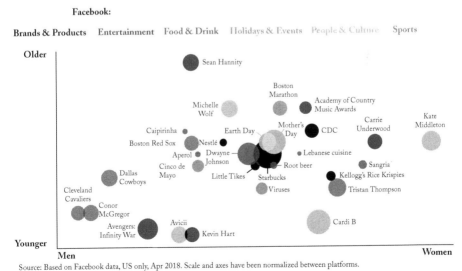

Facebook:

Brands & Products   Entertainment   Food & Drink   Holidays & Events   People & Culture   Sports

Source: Based on Facebook data, US only, Apr 2018. Scale and axes have been normalized between platforms.

Figure 6.1. Most-Discussed Topics on Facebook in April 2018 (Facebook IQ, 2018)

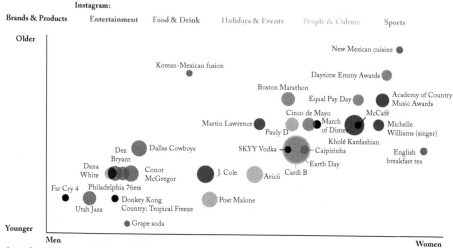

Figure 6.2. Most-Discussed Topics on Instagram in April 2018 (Facebook IQ, 2018)

Both of these lists show that there's still a desire to discuss many forms of media; yet the size of the bubbles in Figures 6.1 and 6.2 report an unintended consequence of making everyone their own media producer: no one can agree as to what the topic should be. People turn to media to find like-minded fans of *Superstore* or the new Jason Isbell album, but struggle to find a critical mass of people in which to interact about these topics in person. The result is a level of loneliness and isolation never before found in the history of social scientific scholarship.

Meanwhile, the work of Twenge (2017) tells us that depression and thoughts of suicide positively correlate with two variables: electronic device usage and television consumption. Meanwhile, five variables were inverse correlates of depression and suicidal thoughts: sports/exercise, reading books/print works, attending religious services, doing homework, and in-person social interactions. One could initially glance at these lists and determine a binary: screens = bad; face-to-face interactions = good. Such a conclusion is fair, but fails to link the two. Consider, for a moment, what people are likely to be interacting *about*. Elements of popular culture inevitably are meant to be touchpoints of cultural conversation. Watercooler programs, for instance, could likewise we referenced as "shows that travel"—from a screen to a face-to-face interaction.

So, using television as that exemplar, let us consider which shows travel the most. The streaming service Netflix is arguably the best mechanism for understanding these core forms of media content desires because of its unmatched number of programmatic offerings. Given the wide range of program lengths, Netflix's unit of analysis—a single streamed minute—is useful for aggregation. Now consider the ten most-viewed programs on Netflix in the year 2018:

Table 6.1. 2018 Top Ten Most-Viewed Programs on Netflix (Sharf, 2019)

Program	Original Network	Years	Minutes (billions)
The Office	NBC	2005–2013	52.1
Friends	NBC	1994–2004	32.6
Grey's Anatomy	ABC	2005-pres	30.3
NCIS	CBS	2003-pres	21.2
Criminal Minds	CBS	2005-pres	19.7
Shameless	Showtime	2011-pres	18.8
Orange is the New Black	Netflix	2013-pres	18.8
Supernatural	WB/CW	2005-pres	18.3
Parks & Recreation	NBC	2009–2015	14.9
Ozark	Netflix	2017-pres	14.0

One could initially notice that only two of the top ten are programs originating on the Netflix platform. One could then dig deeper to discover that the five most popular programs originated 13 or more years from the year of consumption. Yes, more recent shows like *YOU* (Lifetime, Season 1; Netflix Original, Seasons 2 and beyond) and *Riverdale* (CW) built audiences using Netflix, yet these programs still are not consumed at the level of their earlier trailblazers. The modern offerings may be great, but they are not producing any new watercooler programs; they are only making older, established programs more pronounced in that very peaked center of the consumption curve.

Nature Still Abhors a Vacuum

The relatively predictable byproduct of the desire for watercooler discussions combined with a lack of topics in which to discuss is the thought bubble. We find ways (usually online) to find like-minded people, meaning our world gets narrower. Perhaps none offer a better explanation of this process than Lukianoff and Haidt (2018) when they write:

> The media environment … has changed in ways that foster division. Long gone is the time when everybody watched the one of the three national television networks …[since then it's] easy to encase oneself within an echo chamber. And then there's

the 'filter bubble,' in which search engines and YouTube algorithms are designed to give you more of what you seem interested in, leading conservatives and progressives into disconnected moral matrices backed up by mutually contradictory informational worlds. Both the physical and the electronic isolation from people we disagree with allow the forces of confirmation bias, groupthink, and tribalism to push us still further apart (Lukianoff & Haidt, 2018, p. 130–131).

As such forces become part and parcel of the modern mediasphere, we find ourselves back in the place in which Lippmann (1922) described the majority of public opinion stances nearly a century ago, one in which "we do not first see, and then define, we define first and then see" (Lippmann, 1922, Part III, para. 5). When mass media rose to prominence, people could see more and, more critically, witness the same moments in the same way often at the same time. There was a space to see, interpret, and ultimately define—a prospect far more optimal than where one stands particularly in regard to news, where one could define themselves (red team/blue team) and the see information within those lenses.

Those lenses then are magnified by the definition of news sources themselves, seen through the funhouse mirror of everything in a red team (Republican) blue team (Democrat lens) without further distinction. For instance, *The Atlantic* skews left and *The Wall Street Journal* skews right, yet both are considered by most to be legitimate sources of information. The problem happens when each gets places defined not by the reputation of the sources and rather are clustered with other left or right wing options. Suddenly, The Atlantic is aggregated with misleading or fabricated liberal sources, such as *Patribiotics* or *Palmer Report*; *The Wall Street Journal* is aggregated with egregious and troubling sources of conservative information, such as *The Blaze* or *Infowars*. Principles of mood management (see Zillmann, 1988) combine with the "define first/see second" mindset to create distressing current trend lines. A 2019 *Pew* study found that while half of Americans have stopped following a news source because they believed it was advancing false/made up information, 31% click on news stories even with a solid suspicion that the information is fabricated (Mitchell, Gottfried, Stocking, Walker, & Fedeli, 2019). In sum, when there is no Walter Cronkite, no centering or trusted force, all of the niches become questionable to the point that media literacy will take a backseat to desirable news, enjoyed because of the manner in which one identifies, not necessarily because it even is credible.

FOMO, FOBLO, FOBKO: Siblings, Not Twins

As hard as it is to imagine, there was a time when much of our media diets consisted of content people did not overly personally enjoy. Part of this occurred because of scarcity: a finite number of channels, newspaper articles, and radio stations that could come in clearly created what felt like a Hobson's choice for many seeking media that could ably, at a minimum, attract their attention. However, part of the reason people consumed fairly undesirable media was because it was a cultural phenomenon. If you wanted to be at the center of conversation, you could ensure a space by consuming what often fused that conversation together. The result was often an odd mosaic of tastes. In the early 1980s, for instance, that might mean a combination of Robert Ludlum novels, *Dukes of Hazzard* episodes, and films like *Chariots of Fire*. Perhaps the evening news was not the most exciting choice people could select, but it often represented the issues discussed the next day. The relatively limited selection of the options made keeping up manageable; if one did not want to miss out on anything of cultural significance, they likely did not have to do so.

Then choices expanded—rapidly, urgently, and (quite literally) exponentially. Moreover, as each person could become a media producer (using their own devices and social media platforms), cultural import was rivalled and often surpassed by personal import. Sure, one did not wish to be in the dark on the latest trend, meme, or celebrity gossip—but neither did they wish to be left out of the hot restaurant opening in town, a reunion of college friends at a nearby house, or a party hosted by an acquaintance. Including all of these options forged problems in the psyche: the restrictions of time precluded being at all of the places that seemed appealing and also made consuming every touchstone media option impossible, as modern media is "drowning us in content" (Landgraf, para. 1, in Press, 2018)

The result is a heightening of a psychological concept always undergirding social desires: a "fear of missing out", which has developed its own acronym, FOMO, at least partly because of its now ubiquitous use and influence in contemporary society (White, 2013). Social media, argues Dykman (2012) "sets FOMO on fire" (para. 14). A majority (52%) of millennials (age 13–17) experience it when wondering if friends are doing something they are not and a near majority (46%) worry about others finding out information before they do or buying something they have not bought (Dykman, 2012). Milyavskaya, Saffran, Hope, and Koestner (2018) found that FOMO was associated with negative outcomes both daily and over the course of the semester, including increasing negative affect, fatigue, stress, physical symptoms, and decreased sleep. It was also more likely to occur at the end of days or weekends—typically times when people have free time yet are not experiencing the elation they believe they could, bolstered by the fact that 80% of people are using social media to brag about elements of their lives (Dykman, 2012).

In such an environment, though, media (as cultural touchstones) become the bread in the proverbial meat sandwich, with all sorts of other things—typically imagined more than real—forming the meat/core of what people do with their free time. Watching the news, binging a television show, or witnessing what is viral on YouTube becomes what people do when they are not busy making other plans—at least partly because no one is consuming the same media at the same time anymore. *Breaking Bad* ended in 2013 and yet, years later, it is still somehow acceptable for a person to ask that a conversation be muted lest they become victim to a "spoiler alert."

Of course, fear of missing out then has its correlates that, when taken together, help to unpack the true nature of FOMO itself. For instance, there is the "fear of being left out" (FOBLO) as well as the "fear of being kicked out" (FOBKO). Thus, FOMO becomes about the desire we have to bear witness ("I don't want to miss it"), whereas FOBLO is about the desire to belong ("I want to ensure they include me") and FOBKO is more about the inverse ("I want to ensure they don't exclude me"). Considered collectively, the fear of missing out becomes less about the interpersonal watercooler and more about the *credentials* to even be worthy of the watercooler discussion if there is one. FOMO becomes the *antecedent* to the others. After all, one cannot ably discuss who won the debate or the red wedding of *Game of Thrones* unless they watched it, bolstering the chance one is not left out (because they have something to say) or being kicked out (because what they have to say is deemed useful enough to advance the discussion). The sheer amount of time one must dedicate to being the maven: the person who knows about the latest book, Internet meme, or presidential scandal is almost inherently exhausted in the process of keeping up with the latest of the widest media offerings ever to be advanced. One must decide if the prospects of inclusion are worth it, with the ancillary countermovement, dubbed by investment banker Radha Agrawal as the "joy of missing out" (JOMO) as the person who is purposefully detached (Holden, 2018), one who deems the wide demands of unworthy of placing central in life. Inevitably, we could have acronym fatigue or backlash from such concepts: the person tired of FOMO could response with a desire for reclusion, resulting in FOBI (Fear of Being Included) while a person seeking information without interaction might label such desires FONBFK (Fear of Not Being First to Know). As the media evolves in fragmented ways, the manner in which we try to explain psychological responses to such balkanization will proliferate in the process.

Touchpoints Evaporating: An End of the Watercooler Era

In an era of scattered, fragmented media consumption, the downfall of the awards show was an inevitable corollary victim. The 2019 Emmy Awards registered an astonishingly low 6.9 million viewers (Thorne, 2019), down 33% from 2018's previously record low and less than a fifth of the total audience for the highest-viewed Emmys ever in 1986, when 36.8 million viewers tuned in (Fitzgerald, 2018). Depth of the categories was arguably at an all-time high, yet with the massive array of options, worthy winners arose from programs such as Amazon Prime's *Fleabag*, FX's *Pose*, and HBO's *Barry*, programs measuring audiences by the thousands rather than the millions.

The awards show problem is seemingly a universal one, as each are built around watercooler moments predicated on the notion that one nominee is more worthy than another. Those debates are quashed when viewers are unfamiliar with the vast majority of nominees. The Academy Awards briefly flirted with the idea of an "achievement in Popular Film" category before determining it best to put on hold until it could be studied more (VanDerWerff, 2018); those seeking to save the Emmy Awards have sought new categories that are more likely to reward more widely-watched programs on broadcast networks, such as an award for series that produce 18 or more episodes each year (Schneider, 2017). Such remedies still cannot solve the endemic problem: one cannot draw mass audiences for award shows if there are rarely mass audiences for the nominees being honored within them. By the end of 2018, no comedy program could boast an audience of 10 million. The only programs that could even secure one-tenth of the share of the 18–49 viewing demographic were *This Is Us* (for women) and football (for men). Even then, these are small segments of the people already tuning in to television, increasingly then representing a diminishing fraction of a diminishing fraction.

Virtually all media now follows this path. Newspaper circulations have diminished to the point that media scholars McChesney and Pickard (2011) have already declared the "collapse of journalism" while asking "will the last reporter please turn out the lights?" (p. 1). The best- selling book of 2019, Delia Owens's *Where the Crawdads Sing* sold less than one million copies in its first year of release, a far cry from the 8.3 million copies J.K. Rowling's *Harry Potter and the Deathly Hallows* sold in just 24 hours in 2007 (Rich, 2007). Mass media, long thought to have split between traditional and new media models, had ultimately splintered into threads that are nearly impossible to decipher as one uncovers views vs. bounce rates, devices vs. platforms, live vs. time-shifted media consumption.

In such an environment, experiences take precedent over media options because of the communal desires for a shared moment—and the opportunity to say: "I was there" or even, using the *World War Z* Megaticket example, "I was there early." It is the reason why people pay hundreds of dollars for a concert ticket while that same concert, shown later on television, yields a minimal audience. It is the reason increasingly used to attract major donors, letting them enjoy a selfie or phone call with a famous celebrity as a rare experience. It is the reason a company like Hilton expanded its Honors loyalty program in 2019, moving beyond mere free hotel nights and gift cards to backstage passes, golf with a PGA golfer, or the chance to walk the runway with fashion model Winnie Harlow. It is the experience that is prioritized, and media's experiences are too fractured to make others jealous.

In her acclaimed 2018 novel *The Great Believers*, Rebecca Makkai features a character with a profound reflection on the assessment of time:

> If you had to choose when, in the timeline of earth, you got to live—wouldn't you choose the end? You haven't missed anything then. You die in 1920, you miss rock and roll. You die in 1600, you miss Mozart ... the horrors pile up, too, but no one wants to die before the end of the story (Makkai, 2018, p. 382).

The story of media is one with many, many chapters yet to be written. However, what seems abundantly clear is that the story of watercooler mass media is waning, relegated to one-off cases of rare exception—an Avengers movie or Internet meme sprinkled amongst millions of appealing niche products.

This is not to paint a dire future, but certainly to offer a different one in terms of shared experience, cultural touchpoints, and the ability to advance cohesive, agreed upon notions of truth and magnitude. Great—even transcendent—works of journalism and media art will continue to rise in an age where more people have the platform to advance their voice in unique, authentic manners. Still, as our final chapter will attest, navigating this new form of media culture will require a level of media literacy that was not previously required. It will also require mechanisms where niches do not automatically form bubbles and bubbles do not automatically mean echochambers amongst the like-minded and silence amongst the differently-minded. To navigate a media landscape in which the popular is no longer the dominant mechanism for understanding, one must be steadfastly questioning what replaces it—and what these substitutes mean within the larger American landscape.

References

Adler, L. (2016, Feb. 29). New survey reveals 85% of all jobs are filled via networking. *LinkedIn*. Retrieved on March 24, 2020 at: https://www.linkedin.com/pulse/new-survey-reveals-85-all-jobs-filled-via-networking-lou-adler.

Bischoping, K. (1993). Gender differences in conversation topics. *Sex Roles*, 28(1–2), 1–18.

Christley, S. (2017, Aug. 9). The world is shrinking: Six degrees of separation is now 2! *Digital Doughnut*. Retrieved on March 24, 2020 at: https://www.digitaldoughnut.com/articles/2017/august/6-degrees-of-separation-is-now-2.

Cooky, C., Messner, M. A., & Musto, M. (2015). 'It's dude time!' A quarter century of excluding women's sports in televised news and highlight shows. *Communication & Sport, 3*(3), 261–287.

Deming, M. (2013, June 14). Meet the $50 'World War Z' movie ticket: Here's what you get. *Yahoo.* Retrieved on March 24, 2020 at: https://www.yahoo.com/entertainment/bp/meet-50-world-war-z-movie-ticket-162450958.html.

Dykman, A. (2012, Mar. 21). The fear of missing out. *Forbes.* Retrieved on March 24, 2020 at: https://www.forbes.com/sites/moneybuilder/2012/03/21/the-fear-of-missing-out/#2037312d46bd.

Facebook IQ (2018, May 25). Hot topics in the United States for April 2018. Retrieved on March 24, 2020 at: https://www.facebook.com/business/news/insights/2018-04-hot-topics-united-states.

Fisher, N. (2019, Mar. 6). Americans sit more than any time in history and it's literally killing us. *Forbes.* Retrieved on March 24, 2020 at: https://www.forbes.com/sites/nicolefisher/2019/03/06/americans-sit-more-than-anytime-in-history-and-its-literally-killing-us/#6ff0883d779d.

Fitzgerald, T. (2018, Sept. 18). The Emmy Awards by the numbers: Ratings winners, losers, and more. *Forbes.* Retrieved on March 24, 2020 at: https://www.forbes.com/sites/tonifitzgerald/2018/09/18/the-emmy-awards-by-the-numbers-ratings-winners-losers-and-more/#3c2fc07d7c1c.

Gitlin, T. (1980). *The whole world is watching: Mass media in the making and unmaking of the new left.* Berkeley, CA: University of California Press.

Gladwell, M. (2002). *The tipping point: How little things can make a big difference.* Boston, MA: Back Bay Press.

Hibbard, J. (2018, Dec. 13). If you think 2018 had too many shows, here's why. *Entertainment Weekly.* Retrieved on March 24, 2020 at: https://ew.com/tv/2018/12/13/number-tv-shows-2018/.

Holden, L. (2018, Sept. 10). Radha Agrawal can cure your foblo (fear of being left out). *The London Times.* Retrieved on March 24, 2020 at: https://www.thetimes.co.uk/article/radha-agrawal-can-cure-your-foblo-fear-of-being-left-out-vllvjzlhw.

Lanigan, R. (2019, Aug. 5). 25% of millennials don't have a single friend. *Vice.* Retrieved on March 24, 2020 at: https://i-d.vice.com/en_uk/article/kz4epe/millennials-loneliness-friendships?utm_source=dmfb.

Lippmann, W. (1922). *Public opinion.* New York: Harcourt Brace.

Lukianoff, G., & Haidt, J. (2018). *The coddling of the American mind.* New York: Penguin.

Luscombe, B. (2019, Oct. 14). 10 questions: Bob Iger. *Time ,97*, p. 60.

Makkai, R. (2018). *The great believers.* New York: Viking.

Maven, M. (2019, Feb. 21). $22 million made by a 7-year old's 1 big idea. *Forbes.* Retrieved on March 24, 2020 at: https://www.forbes.com/sites/michaelmaven/2019/02/21/exposed-22-million-made-by-a-7-year-old-with-1-shocking-big-idea/#410d58fe2ed6.

McChesney, R. W., & Pickard, V. (Eds.) (2011). *Will the last reporter please turn out the lights: The collapse of journalism and what can be done to fix it.* New York: The New Press.

Michos, E. D. (2019). Sitting disease: How a sedentary lifestyle affects heart health. *Johns Hopkins Medicine.* Retrieved on March 24, 2020 at: https://www.hopkinsmedicine.org/health/wellness-and-prevention/sitting-disease-how-a-sedentary-lifestyle-affects-heart-health.

Milgram, S. (1967). The small world problem. *Psychology Today, 2,* 60–67.

Milyavskaya, M., Saffran, M., Hope, N., & Koestner, R. (2018). Fear of missing out: Prevalence, dynamics, and consequences of experiencing FOMO. *Motivation and Emotion, 42*(5), 725–737.

Mitchell, A., Gottfried, J., Stocking, G., Walker, M., & Fedeli, S. (2019, June 5). Many Americans say that made up news is a critical problem that needs to be fixed. *Pew Research Center.* Retrieved on March 24, 2020 at: https://www.journalism.org/2019/06/05/political-leaders-activists-viewed-as-prolific-creators-of-made-up-news-journalists-seen-as-the-ones-to-fix-it/#most-have-taken-steps-in-response-to-made-up-news.

Murthy, V. (2017). Work and the loneliness epidemic. *Harvard Business Review, 9.* Retrieved on March 24, 2020 at: https://hbr.org/cover-story/2017/09/work-and-the-loneliness-epidemic.

National Association of Theatre Owners (2019). Number of U.S. movie screens. Retrieved on March 24, 2020 at: https://www.natoonline.org/data/us-movie-screens/.

OfCom (2017, Aug. 3). Box set Britain: UK's TV and online habits revealed. Retrieved on March 24, 2020 at: https://www.ofcom.org.uk/about-ofcom/latest/media/media-releases/2017/box-set-britain-tv-online-habits.

Press, J. (2018, Aug. 3). Peak TV is still drowning us in content, says TV prophet John Landgraf. *Vanity Fair.* Retrieved on March 24, 2020 at: https://www.vanityfair.com/hollywood/2018/08/peak-tv-fxjohn-landgraf-tca-donald-glover-chris-rock.

Rich, M. (2007, July 22). Record first-day sales for last 'Harry Potter' book. *The New York Times.* Retrieved on March 24, 2020 at: https://www.nytimes.com/2007/07/22/books/22cnd-potter.html.

Rubenking, B. Bracken, C. C., Sandoval, J., & Rister, A. (2018). Defining new viewing behaviours: What makes and motivates TV binge-watching? *International Journal of Digital Television, 9*(1), 69–85.

Schneider, M. (2017, July 11). Emmys anger: Why the TV academy should consider these new categories to recognize more shows. *IndieWire.* Retrieved on March 24, 2020 at: https://www.indiewire.com/2017/07/emmys-television-academy-categories-best-new-series-1201853967/.

Schulze, H. (2018, Apr. 16). Loneliness: An epidemic? *Harvard University's Promoting Public Health.* Retrieved on March 24, 2020 at: http://sitn.hms.harvard.edu/flash/2018/loneliness-an-epidemic/?ncid=APPLENEWS00001.

Sharf, Z. (2019, Apr. 24). Netflix users are spending more time streaming 'The Office' than any other show—report. *Indiewire.* Retrieved on March 24, 2020 at: https://www.indiewire.com/2019/04/the-office-netflix-most-streamed-series-friends-1202127682/

Smith, C. (2019, Aug. 5). Netflix statistics 2019: How many subscribers does Netflix have? *Business Statistics.* Retrieved on March 24, 2020 at: https://expandedramblings.com/index.php/netflix_statistics-facts/.

Thorne, W. (2019, Sept. 23). TV ratings: Emmy awards sink 33% to record low. *Variety*. Retrieved on March 24, 2020 at: https://variety.com/2019/tv/news/emmy-ratings-2019-awards-show-1203345607/.

Twenge, J. (2017). *iGen: Why today's super-connected kids are growing up less rebellious, more tolerant, less happy—and completely unprepared for adulthood—and what that means for the rest of us*. New York: Atria Books.

VanDerWerff, E. T. (2018, Sept. 6). The Oscars are killing the new 'popular film' category-for now. *Vox*. Retrieved on March 24, 2020 at: https://www.vox.com/culture/2018/9/6/17828204/oscars-popular-film-canceled-dead.

White, J. (2013, July 8). Research finds link between social media and the 'fear of missing out.' *The Washington Post*. Retrieved on March 24, 2020 at: https://www.washingtonpost.com/national/health-science/research-finds-link-between-social-media-and-the-fear-of-missing-out/2013/07/08/b2cc7ddc-e287-11e2-a11e-c2ea876a8f30_story.html.

Zillmann, D. (1988). Mood management through communication choices. *American Behavioral Scientist, 31*(3), 327–341.

CHAPTER SEVEN

Media Balkanization Theory: Axioms and Implications

This book has traversed quite a bit of ground, showing that population growth and advances in communication technology have shifted dramatically since the peak of mass communication, shown in Chapter 1. However, we explain in Chapter 2, as content sources proliferated over the last decade or so (especially on the Internet and social media) the once mass audience became balkanized into smaller and often heterogeneous niche audiences. These audience fragments consume different constellations of media sources and, therefore, acquire different information and develop different attitudes because rhetoric is epistemic. The way human beings process information (the primacy of affect, congruency bias, disconfirmation bias) leads these balkanized audiences to have different world views: varying beliefs and values, and concomitantly conflicting attitudes, contrasting ideologies, different voting behavior. The repeated refrain of "fake news" leads some voters to reject disconfirming information when they do encounter it. Chapter 3 then applied some of the same principles of balkanization to entertainment media, highlighting how the different constellations play out in regard to the music we listen to, the books we read, the scripted programs and movies that we watch, and well beyond. Chapters 4, 5, and 6 then unfurled the ramifications of this balkanization, ranging from what has been added (customization, in Chapter 4), what has been redefined (cultural barometers, in Chapter 5), and what has been lost (watercooler moments, in Chapter 6).

In this final chapter, we discuss several observations about the balkanization of the mass media, offering our media balkanization theory. As we noted before, we do not make the claim that no overlap exists in the beliefs and attitudes of fragmented audiences, only that the homogeneity that was once created by the mass media has dissipated. This plays out in a variety of mediated capacities, yet, we argue, the axioms of media balkanization hold whether referencing news, sports, or other forms of entertainment. We do not examine media balkanization in other countries but we anticipate this phenomenon is not limited to the United States.

Media Balkanization Theory

This chapter lays out the basics of our media balkanization theory. We articulate six axioms undergirding our theory. Next, we discuss the implications of media balkanization for several communication theories including Image Repair Theory (Benoit, 2015) and the functional theory of political campaign discourse (see, e.g. Benoit, 2007, 2014a, 2014b). Finally, we apply our approach to two exemplars, first in the news context, helping understand President Donald Trump's popularity with his base, and second in the entertainment context, explaining the enduring appeal of Netflix (and other competing streaming services).

The core of media balkanization postulates that the fragmentation of the mass media audience into niche groups forces reinterpretation of the majority of our core media theories, particularly effect-based theories. The *amount* of content has exploded while the human capacity (measured in both *time* and *attention*) has not (and cannot, because of the limited attention span of a human being) expand along with the bloat of media content. Undergirding the theory are six key axioms:

A1. In the past, increases in population and advances in communication technology fueled the growth of the mass media.

A2. More recently, further communication technological advances—particularly cable TV, the Internet, and social media—have created new content sources and fragmented the mass audience.

A3. As the number of content sources proliferates, these new outlets often have an incentive to narrow their content, hoping to attract smaller, more homogeneous, and more loyal niche audiences for that outlet.

A4. Because mass media effects are proportional to audience size, as the audience for a given medium shrinks, the potential influence from media effects decreases.

A5. For theories of media that focus more broadly on content (e.g. cultivation theory, uses and gratifications): media balkanization has less impact.

A6. Choice of content sources is influenced by the uses and gratifications sought by potential auditors as well as other variables (such as ideology).

Chapter 1 provides support for the first axiom. Chapter 2 makes our case for the second and third axioms. We develop the final three axioms next.

Some Mass Media Effects Are Proportional to Size of Audience

The fourth axiom asserts that some mass media effects are proportional to audience size. This claim should be self-evident: The more (fewer) people who are exposed to a medium the greater (smaller) are the effects on that audience. We will illustrate this idea with two theories: agenda-setting and framing theory (see Benoit & Holbert, 2010; Scheufele, 2000); we believe it is also true for priming.

Agenda-setting theory investigates how public opinion about the relative importance of policy issues shifts over time. Cohen (1963) declared that media "may not be successful much of the time in telling people what to think [what attitudes to embrace], but it is stunningly successful in telling its readers what to think about" (p. 13). Thus, agenda-setting is about how audiences perceive the relative importance or salience of issues such as energy, the environment, immigration, or employment. McCombs and Shaw (1972) established that when an issue is repeatedly discussed by the news, the audience perceives that issue to be more important (see also McCombs, 2004; Wanta & Ghanem, 2007). However, contemporary fragmented media messages stress different issues (i.e., have different content)—particularly in today's politically divisive environment—which reduces the ability of repetition to affect the salience of an issue. Of course, some overlap in issue discussion still occurs today, but in a balkanized media environment a smaller number of people in niche audiences are exposed to a given issue repeatedly, compared with a true mass media. McCombs explained that "the redundancy across outlets that has characterized mass communication for many decades will be greatly reduced as new media offer very different agendas" (2004, p. 147). McCombs wrote this 15 years ago; in the meantime, media balkanization increased the heterogeneity of content sources and of content. The agenda-setting power of the media is curtailed as more people consume different constellations of media which emphasize different content. The agenda-setting effect can still occur, but it happens to fewer people in smaller audiences. Instead of a mass media promoting an issue agenda, we have multiple media promoting varying issue agendas.

Framing theory (see, e.g. Goffman, 1974; Gamson & Modigliani, 1987; Iyengar, 1991) assumes that people can view a person, organization, or event from different perspectives. These interpretative frames or perspectives can influence attitudes. Entman (1993) observed that frames can "promote a particular problem definition, causal interpretation, moral evaluation, and/or treatment recommendation" (p. 52). An elected official's words and deeds can be viewed from the perspective that he or she is a politician (merely pandering to voters) or as a statesman/ stateswoman (working to benefit his or her electorate). Another example of a contrast in frames can be seen in ideas about poverty. This condition can be understood as a result of laziness or structural limitations (education, opportunities). These two perspectives on poverty imply markedly different solutions. How one understands problems in the world influences the solutions that appear appropriate. When mass audiences become balkanized, fewer people are exposed to a given frame. As with agenda-setting, framing can still occur, but is limited to far smaller audiences. It is likely that repeated exposure to niche media with similar content could have larger framing effects for audiences.

Media Theories That Are Less Constrained by Balkanized Media

Our fifth axiom argues that some theories of mass communication are less dependent on audience size for their importance. We embrace uses and gratifications theory in Chapter 2. The basic idea—that people choose which messages to attend based in part on how they use media and the gratifications they obtain from media. As media balkanize, the fragmented media may make it easier to find media that match well with our desires. We think media balkanization has relatively little impact on U&G, other than making the concept of niche gratification theory (see Dimmick, 2003) more relevant as more choices amount to a greater opportunity to get precise matches of uses sought and gratifications obtained. U&G theory does not argue that particular uses or gratifications are equally important for all audiences, just that mass audiences have been largely replaced with niche audiences.

Cultivation theory may also not be particularly limited by today's fragmented media. This theory argues that consumption of mass media "cultivates" consumers' perception of reality (Gerbner & Gross, 1972). The "mean world hypothesis" holds that people who watch more TV shows with violent content (including crime dramas) are likely to believe the world is a dangerous place than other viewers. For example, people who watch more violent TV programming are likely to overestimate the actual amount of crime in society. The balkanization of the mass media is not likely to have a huge influence on cultivation theory because this theory conceptualizes media content at a different level from other theories. For instance, people may still see "mean world" visualizations through violent programming, even if the number of violent programming options is way more plentiful than before. People might have to consume different messages to form mean world conceptions, but the ability for cultivation through heavy exposure remains relatively constant. In contrast to agenda-setting (McCombs & Shaw, 1972) and issue ownership (Petrocik, 1996; Petrocik, Benoit, & Hansen, 2003–2004), which are interested in particular issues such as crime, taxation, or unemployment, cultivation concerns more general media content, violent content or similar consistently consumed representations. People who have a proclivity for violent content should have little trouble finding such content after balkanization. In fact, with so many content sources available, it is even easier to find content that can be cultivated now than at the height of mass media, whether that be violence, sex, or other heuristics people use to understand society through mediation.

Although we clearly embrace U&G, this theory is not designed to explain why Democrats and Republicans choose different media to satisfy their desires, although it is possible that liberals and conservatives tend to seek different gratifications from the messages they consume. Ideology can explain part of media choice, but one could identify a variety of factors that play a role in media choice. For example, alumni of one university may choose to watch different football (or basketball) games than people who attended other universities. People may choose to watch comedies over action/adventure movies and yet still seek the same gratification: diversion.

Implications of Balkanization Theory for Image Repair Theory

Given our publication history, the question arises of the implications of balkanization for Image Repair Theory (see, e.g. Benoit, 2015). This theory recognizes the fact that criticism (attacks, complaints) are inevitable in human interaction. Image Repair Theory discusses the antecedents of defensive discourse and identifies verbal strategies for repairing a damaged image, arguing that defensive messages should actually focus on the accusations and attempt to reach the target audience. It is a waste of time and resources to try to reach people who are not important to the defender. So, if a defender needs to repair its audience with a more general audience, it may be more difficult (or costly) to reach that audience after media have been fragmented. On the other hand, if the defender needs to persuade a limited audience, balkanization may make image repair a bit easier because fragmented audiences tend to be relatively homogeneous and less difficult to target with their image repair messages. This fragmentation could also mean that attacks which occur on a source with niche content may reach the relevant audience more easily than before. Balkanization does not affect the assumptions of the theory or the options it identifies for repairing an image.

Implications of Balkanization Theory for the Functional Theory of Campaign Discourse

We also address the implications of media balkanization for the theory of political campaign discourse (see, e.g. Benoit, 2007, 2014a, 2014b). This theory argues that the function of election messages is to persuade voters that one candidate is preferable to opponents. This function can be achieved through three message strategies: acclaims (identification and emphasis of the candidate's pros), attacks (identification and emphasis of the opponent's cons) and defenses (refutations) of criticism of the source. These three functions can occur on two possible topics: character (the kind of person the candidate is) and policy (the political actions the candidate would take if elected). Politics concerns controversial issues so it is not possible to persuade *all* voters (or all citizens who cast votes) that one candidate is a better choice than the other. Luckily, candidates need not convince all voters of their superiority (a majority of voters in states that have 270 electoral votes). The fact that audiences have fragmented may make it easier and/or less expensive to target particular segments of the electorate. If, as we argue, conservatives have a proclivity for using conservative media (and if liberals tend to consume liberal media) the effects of ideologically-based messages may be intensified. Again, balkanization does not change the three functions, two topics, or the predictions of functional theory.

News Balkanization: Today's Fragmented Media Enables President Trump

President Donald Trump offers quite a puzzle. Paraphrasing Winston Churchill's declaration about Russia in 1939: He "is a riddle, wrapped in a mystery, inside an enigma." In 2016, people did not expect Donald Trump to win the Republican nomination or the Electoral College (he lost the popular vote of the general election by almost three million votes; see, e.g. Benoit & Glantz, 2020). One could have predicted—both because he identified most recently as a Republican and was known as a business mogul—that he would cut taxes. On the other hand, we do not think most could have anticipated has actions toward North Korea, for example, or toward our traditional world allies such as England or France. Issue ownership principles could ask why so many conservatives continue to support this president when he repeatedly disrespects the military (Collinson, 2019).

Yet somehow, through it all, he retained much of his support among voters. From January 2017 through November of 2019, his approval rating varied between 35% and 44% (Gallup, 2019; time will eventually tell if the coronavirus pandemic would be his downfall). President Trump's relatively stable approval rating contrasts sharply with, for example, President George W. Bush, whose approval fluctuated between 25% and 90%. As noted in Chapter 2, the President's approval rating is very high among Republicans.

Observers have documented a myriad of lies told by the president. For example, Kiely, Robertson, Farley, and Gore (2019) provide several examples of the President's falsehoods from one day in October of 2019:

> In two press appearances in the same day, President Donald Trump made several false claims and distorted the facts on issues ranging from Syria to trade:
>
> > Trump claimed that former GOP House Speaker Paul Ryan "would never issue a subpoena," because of his "respect for our country." But subpoenas were issued under Ryan's watch. "Our committee alone issued more than 100 subpoenas," a former GOP House oversight staffer has said.
> >
> > Trump said "the FBI never got" the DNC server that was hacked during the 2016 election, and that the server is now held by a company co-owned by someone "from Ukraine." But the company—which is based in the U.S.—gave the FBI an exact copy of the DNC hard drives. It also has said it never possessed the servers and that its owners are not from Ukraine ....
> >
> > Trump again distorted the facts about the whistleblower report's account of his July 25 phone call with the president of Ukraine. The White House-released rough transcript of the call supported what the whistleblower said ....
> >
> > While boasting about the performance of the stock market, Trump repeated the false claim that "all people own in the stock markets." Only about half of Americans own stock, directly or indirectly.

In fact, journalists who perform fact checks conclude that he lied throughout his presidency. For example, the *Washington Post* reported that while in office President Donald Trump has made 15,413 "false or misleading claims" by the middle of December 2019 (Kessler, Rizzo, & Kelly, 2019). The Associated Press (2019) provided an example of a Trump lie from November 2019.

President Donald Trump persists in his false story that he opened an Apple manufacturing plant last week. Trump, looking back at his Nov. 20 trip to Austin, Texas: "I opened up an Apple computer plant."—Florida rally Tuesday.

THE FACTS: He didn't do that. He visited an Austin factory that's been making the Mac Pro for Apple since 2013. He made the same claim in a tweet the day of his visit: "Today I opened a major Apple Manufacturing plant in Texas that will bring high paying jobs back to America."

This statement finds the President taking credit for creating jobs that were actually created six years prior. Leonhardt and Thompson (2017) concluded that:

There is simply no precedent for an American president to spend so much time telling untruths. Every president has shaded the truth or told occasional whoppers. No other president—of either party—has behaved as Trump is behaving. He is trying to create an atmosphere in which reality is irrelevant.

Notice that the idea that reality is irrelevant means that the thesis that rhetoric is epistemic is very powerful indeed. Still, how can supporters trust a person who lies so often?

It is surely the case that a variety of reasons can be offered for Donald Trump's victory in the Electoral College as well as his current popularity among supporters. For example, some people resent (if not outright dislike) immigrants. Regardless of whether the "Wall" is built—and whether Mexico pays for it—the President's anti-immigrant sentiments may very well appeal to these voters. Some people desire lower taxes; President Trump (and Congress) delivered "bigly" to this audience. Some Americans believe the U.S. is the victim of bad trade agreements. Trump's policies (particularly tariffs) probably appeal to these folks. Some voters liked his persona as a Washington outsider, a business magnate, and a person who prides himself on flaunting the expectations of political correctness. These are all controversial questions and other voters disagree.

Media balkanization theory provides further insight into his continued popularity with his base in addition to their agreements with his policy positions and liking of his persona. As shown in Chapter 2, liberals and conservatives have conflicting perceptions of the accuracy of network reporting. Generally, Republicans have different media diets than Democrats. This means that Trump supporters use, and are enveloped by, a media environment of messages emanating from the President and his supporters that promote President Trump, his actions, and his statements. These messages reinforce one another and promulgate a particular world view (see Jamieson & Cappella, 2008, on Rush Limbaugh and the echo chamber). The hostile media effect and the GOP's constant hammering of "fake news" can lead conservatives to reject messages that conflict with their belief system. Of course, Democrats promulgate a different world view, and develop their understanding of the world from a different constellation of content sources but this section of the chapter is about the President and his supporters so it is the stark contrast that is of most note to media balkanization theory. To wit, it is not that the truth of the claim of 15,413 lies the *Washington Post* reports cannot be debated or whether they were innocent errors or mild exaggerations; those types of distinctions were present even at the peak of mass communication. The difference is now in the repetition of statements by respected sources and the occurrence of rebuttal: Fox Business host Stuart Varney counters the 13,345 with a new total: zero, arguing that he never lies, only "exaggerates" (Hutzler, 2019). That type of gap between realities is, indeed, something new—and a byproduct of media balkanization.

As noted, a staple of political journalism is fact checking (attempts to inform citizens of the veracity or falsity of statements made by many public figures, especially the President) these journalists have done a "land office business" checking statements by President Trump. In a traditional mass media environment such concerns about a president would reach most voters. However, in an ideologically fragmented environment people who get most or all of their news from conservative media (1) are less likely to be exposed to these fact checks and (2) are continually exposed to the President's defenses of his statements and policies. Conservative sources also repeat the president's defenses (e.g. "there was no quid pro quo"). Furthermore, Trump's repeated refrain of "fake news" is echoed by other conservatives, conservative media, and social media. Similarly, voters who mainly consume liberal media are less likely to be exposed to pro-Trump messages and more likely to consume messages that criticize the president.

Repeated claims of "fake news" by the President and his supporters tend to undermine unfavorable claims made about Trump advanced in fact checks with his base. If a Trump supporter accidentally encounters criticisms of the president in news media (or elsewhere), they have a ready-made reason to reject those criticisms: These criticisms are fake. Recall that in December of 2019 the Trump campaign created a webpage explicitly focused on promoting and defending the president (www.snowflakevictory.com, discussed in Chapter 2).

Furthermore, the way people process the information from messages they encounter (the primacy of affect, congruence bias, disconfirmation bias) tends to reinforce the attitudes of both liberals and conservatives. Once a voter has developed a favorable attitude toward Donald Trump, those attitudes influence how they process messages from and about him. Our point is not to revisit the rise of candidate Trump in 2016, but the fact that he had no experience before the Republican primaries and thus few people had negative attitudes toward him.

Among the first information they acquired about this candidate were ideas like "build a wall—and make Mexico pay for it," he self-funded his primary campaign so he was free from special interests, he was ready to speak his mind (implicitly rejecting political correctness). As he rose in the polls, other Republicans began to take him seriously and attack him. But the basic foundation for some voters had already begun to be established and these pro-Trump ideas and attitudes influenced how voters reacted to these criticisms. The fact that these ideas are repeated so many times matters because (1) message repetition increases that message's persuasiveness and (2) because rhetoric is epistemic, works to create a social reality supporting Donald Trump.

Entertainment Balkanization: Customization and Expansion as Precursor for Netflix Dominance

As this book argues, balkanization applies to more than just news, altering each media ecosystem in different (yet related) ways. Chapter 6 explained the odd case of Netflix, a service in which the majority of Americans now subscribe (a modern rarity), and yet providing original content that, while highly desired by its customers, nevertheless is secondary to the older network shows it provides. No Netflix Original offering can match viewership of old episodes of *Criminal Minds* or *Grey's Anatomy* that draws even more viewership on the platform.

Here, Netflix becomes an exemplar of how the final three axioms of the theory can intermingle in the world of entertainment. Media effects postulate diminished impact, media content postulates largely stay the same, and content choice (uses and gratifications) become more specialized.

First, it is difficult to argue that any single Netflix offering has the amount of media effects that other past content offerings possessed. As we have previously noted, Netflix offers high numbers of total accounts that "have viewed" a specific program or movie, but often the number of people completing it is less than 20%. As such, noting that over 40 million accounts watched "some" of the third season of *Stranger Things* does not tell us much. Application of the 20% metric could mean that as few as eight million people finished the first episode. Moreover, given that part of media effects occur in the post-viewing discussions and debates, rarely do these shows qualify as mass communication; one person binges a show over the first weekend while other might discover it months or even years later. For Netflix, the potential audience is quite high, but the actual audience is spread so thin among its many high-quality offerings that no single program can rise to watercooler status.

Regarding the theory's fifth axiom, that content-oriented theories would be less affected by media balkanization, the principle holds for Netflix because, for instance, cultivation still occurs as people still seek shows, watch them deeply, and find that media sets the terms of debate for societal interactions. The ability to binge-watch changes this equation (via shorter yet more intense viewing sessions), altering the way we interact with media (Pittman & Sheehan, 2015) and causing different viewer experiences via time-shifting (Conlin, Billings, & Auverset, 2016). However, in terms of sheer exposure to media content, the limits of human viewing capacity result in overall exposure to professionally-produced, broadly-defined media content stays largely flat (Madrigal, 2018). Yes, Americans utilize screens more than ever before, yet it is because of other elements of online entertainment (individuals a media producers for social media platforms, paying bills, and facilitating human interactions) that account for this, not a spike (or drop) in entertainment media consumed.

However, the uses and gratifications function of navigating media content has changed from its ubiquity and niche elements. One could now determine not just what *types* of content to consume, but the *manner* in which they would wish to consume it. Before, one could ask another the question: have you seen the movie about "X" and people could utilize heuristics to connect and form a conversation. Now, each content possibility has considerable nuance with a multitude of offerings. If one wanted to watch the offering about the Fox News sexual harassment scandal, there was Showtime's *The Loudest Voice* or the film offering *Bombshell*. If one wishes to have Fox News infused themes but not have it be about Fox News, there HBO's *Succession* could fit the bill. Similarly, the Me Too movement could be chronicled in very short bursts of information (via #metoo movement on social media), series form (via the Apple+ program, *The Morning Show*) or extended book form (via Ronan Farrow's 464-page tome, *Catch and Kill*). Much as one could now differentiate news on a variety of continua (political slant, journalism vs. discussion, outrage vs. serene), entertainment unfolds in the same manner with nuanced wormholes at virtually every term. Whether one likes Marvel content is no longer as pertinent as what types of Marvel content one follows. Axiom 6 of the theory highlights the degree of customization and fragmentation that pervades both news and entertainment, in similar yet distinctive manners.

Conclusion

We initially wrote this conclusion to our book at the end of 2019. All of our the postulates held. News was so balkanized that parts of the news claimed Trump's impeachment was the easiest case to establish in American history while other parts claim it was entirely manufactured. Music was so balkanized that no current release moved the needle, resulting Billboard's #1 song in America being a 1994 Mariah Carey Christmas anthem, "All I Want for Christmas is You," immediately followed by Brenda Lee's 1958 classic "Rocking Around the Christmas Tree," both eclipsing their previous chart peaks decades after release; the songs were never mountains on the charts—until 2019, when no mountains were left to surmount. Scripted television is so balkanized that the new CBS sitcom *The Unicorn* was considered a standout hit for garnering 5.7 million viewers, a rating that would have trailed all but four network programs and five daytime soap operas 30 years ago. Masses were still using media, yet with what we consider "mass communication" rarely occurring. It was all customized, targeted, and designed to please each person in their own unique way.

Then came coronavirus (COVID-19). The World Health Organization declared the corona virus outbreak to be a pandemic on March 11, 2020 (Gumbrecht & Howard, 2020). Public schools, colleges, universities were then closed thoughout the country (Levenson, Boyette, & Mack, 2020) before largely moving to online/distance educational formats. All sports were largely shut down except for transactional events such as free agent signings that could be conducted remotely. Many other public events, such as St. Patrick's Day parades, Coachella and Stagecoach music festivals, and marathons were cancelled or postponed. In many places gatherings of more than 10 people were shut down. These responses to this dangerous and widespread disease are certain to have implications for media use. Millions of people replaced attendance at public events with greater use of social media and other content sources. At their best, customized niche media combined with informed social media to facilitate practices like social distancing. At their worst, these same media sources accelerated spread, with false information and the politicization of the pandemic as a hoax. Furthermore, the extreme levels of uncertainty and continuing changes in response to COVID-19 were certain to increase use of social media and other content sources to seek information about the growing threat.

This book has chronicled the rise of a relatively homogeneous mass media, fueled by population growth and new communication technologies. However, introduction of multiple media—particularly the Internet and social media—balkanized the mass media into niche content sources with smaller, more heterogeneous audiences. As we argue particularly in this final chapter, this development has implications for the majority of mass communication theories. Using six key axioms, we addressed the implications of media balkanization for several theories, such as agenda setting and framing. We also use our theory to provide a perspective on attitudes toward President Donald Trump in his base as well as to explain the ubiquity of appeals for streaming content, most notably Netflix.

We wish to end by addressing one final question: Is media balkanization a good thing or a bad thing—or both? We believe that, in general, more choices are desirable—particularly when the user's motive is entertainment. Twenty years ago, those who loved cooking, or sports, or country music, or history, or home improvement, and so forth, had relatively few opportunities to view such content on their televisions. You did not get to choose *what* cooking show or sports contest you wished to watch; you basically watched *whatever* was available in the genre. Now, viewers have immense options for entertainment and many more in each of these classifications.

On the information/persuasion side, those who send persuasive messages (such as politicians or advertisers) presumably find getting their messages in front of their intended audiences much easier to do than in past media ecosystems. Media balkanazation helps companies, organizations, and individuals who seek to persuade, as well as marketers. Persuasion becomes highly efficient today (even while the given message itself is not necessarily more persuasive). Those who sell, for example, baldness treatments probably do not seek to reach children and do not enjoy paying for their messages to reach those who are highly unlikely to purchase their product. Tax preparation firms presumably do not benefit from paying to send their messages to billionaires (who already have personalized tax consultants). Balkanization helps with micro-targeting, and that proves useful for many stakeholders.

However, people who seek information about candidates, politicians, and policy questions are much more often informed today by ideologically biased content sources, including webpages and social media. In an ideologically balkanized media, voters are likely to be exposed to news that is slanted to the right or the left and, perhaps more problematically, will be unexposed to news that does not hew to one's ideology. The existence of both left wing and right wing social media does not mean people are exposed to balanced information (people will frequently follow right wing or left wing messages but not both). It is much less likely today for voters to hear or see both sides of an issue discussed, enabling informed choices. This is not healthy for our democracy. As Delli Carpini and Keeter (1996) observe, "democracy functions best when its citizens are politically informed" (p. 1). Being well-informed with ideologically biased information is not the ideal state of affairs.

We also do not see a way for further technological advances to dramatically change this situation: once voters have a choice to consume ideologically biased media, many are unlikely to seek out information that conflicts with their attitudes and values. Freud's Pleasure Principle postulates that humans are driven to seek pleasure and avoid pain; the principle seemingly holds true in the case of ideological media. In fact, the evidence on media use presented in Chapter 2 demonstrated that news consumers from the left and the right are prone to use different content sources—with different content. We do not want to overstate our case: Some people do consume a diet of content sources which expressing contrasting viewpoints. However, we find it impossible to doubt that many more people are exposed to ideologically biased information now than was the case 20 or 30 years ago. Even when people expose themselves to multiple viewpoints, those often place a piece of fact along with a contrasting misnomer.

We see two possibilities for improvement here. First, congress could enact legislation requiring that news media present more than one side of every issue they report. This seems highly unlikely and we think it would be impossible to police, especially with content source on the Internet including social media. It also would not present utopia in any demonstrable form; a climate change debate can occur, yet every scientific study need not be accompanied by a scant minority of contrasting scientific opinions of dubious repute. Moreover, not all issues have two viable sides: a piece on the dangers of anorexia, for instance, need not be balanced with a representative from the pro-anorexia (pro-ana) movement. Thus, the first option is not practical or viable. A second possible remedy to balkanization would occur if the U.S. faces a terrible crisis, such as a war or increasingly obvious problems from climate change. When stakes are heightened, ideology might be devalued in the desire for pragmatic remedies. Such a circumstance (perhaps the coronavirus pandemic) might draw people together. Of course, we do not hope for a crisis to befall America. So, we believe ideological media balkanization to continue for the foreseeable future, perhaps even growing worse. It seems likely that the ideological divide among voters will continue and perhaps even deepen.

Most, including your two authors, would say that media balkanization has some wonderful benefits. Yet, each media diet is now the functional equivalent of a snowflake, with few matching elements that fused common understandings of information, emotion, and the human experience. Most, including your two authors, would say that is problematic. Both can be simultaneously true and debated; what cannot, based on virtually every metric offered in this book, is that mass communication has risen and fallen and now we must endeavor to figure out what could and should happen next.

References

AP. (2019, November 26). AP fact check: Trump and the Apple plant he didn't open. Accessed 12/3/19: https://apnews.com/3355fbf1965d47559f036844434cdaf8.

Benoit, W. L. (2007). *Communication in political campaigns.* New York: Peter Lang.

Benoit, W. L. (2014a). *A functional analysis of political television advertisements* (2nd ed.). Lanham, MD: Lexington Books.

Benoit, W. L. (2014b). *Political election debates: Informing voters about policy and character.* Lanham, MD: Lexington Books.

Benoit, W. L. (2015). *Accounts, excuses, apologies: Image repair theory and research* (2nd ed.). Albany: State University of New York Press.

Benoit, W. L., & Glantz, M. J. (2020). *Presidential campaigns in the age of social media: Clinton and Trump.* New York: Peter Lang.

Benoit, W. L., & Holbert, R. L. (2010). Political communication. In C. R. Berger, M. E. Roloff, & D. R. Roskos-Ewoldsen (Eds.), *Handbook of communication science* (2nd ed., pp. 437–452). Thousand Oaks, CA: Sage.

Churchill, W. (1939, October 1). The Russian enigma. *The Churchill Society.* Accessed 12//9/19: http://www.churchill-society-london.org.uk/RusnEnig.html.

Cohen, B. (1963). *The press and foreign policy.* Princeton: Princeton University Press.

Collinson, S. (2019, January 1). Trump says he loves the military, but he keeps insulting its members. *CNN.* Accessed 1/2/20: https://www.cnn.com/2018/11/20/politics/donald-trump-william-mcraven-military/index.html.

Conlin, L. T., Billings, A. C., & Auverset, L. A. (2016). Time-shifting vs. appointment viewing: The role of fear of missing out within TV consumption habits. *Communication & Society, 29*(4), 151–164.

Delli Carpini, M. X., & Keeter, S. (1996). *What Americans know about politics and why it matters.* New Haven, CT: Yale University.

Dimmick, J. (2003). *Media competition and coexistence: The theory of the niche.* Mahwah, NJ: Lawrence Erlbaum Associates.

Entman, R. (1993). Framing: Toward a clarification of a fractured paradigm. *Journal of Communication, 43*, 51–58.

Gallup Poll (2019). Presidential approval ratings—Donald Trump. Accessed 12/9/19: https://news.gallup.com/poll/203198/presidential-approval-ratings-donald-trump.aspx.

Gamson, W. A., & Modigliani, A. (1987). The changing culture of affirmative action. In R.G. Braungart & M. M. Braungart (Eds.), Research in Political Sociology, *3*, 137–177.

Gerbner, G. & Gross, L. (1972). Living with television: The violence profile. *Journal of Communication, 26*, 173–199.

Goffman, E. (1974). *Frame analysis.* New York: Harper & Row.

Gumbrecht, J., & Howard, J. (2020, March 11). WHO declares novel coronavirus outbreak a pandemic. CNN. Accessed 3/12/20: https://www.cnn.com/2020/03/11/health/coronavirus-pandemic-world-health-organization/index.html.

Hutzler, A. (2019, August 30). Fox Business host tells Trump 2020 challenger that he has never lied: 'he exaggerates and spins.' *Newsweek.* Retrieved at: https://www.newsweek.com/fox-business-host-says-trump-has-never-lied-1457038.

Iyengar, S. (1991). *Is anyone responsible? How television frames political issues.* Chicago: University of Chicago Press.

Jamieson, K. H., & Cappella, J. N. (2008). *Echo chamber: Rush Limbaugh and the conservative media establishment*. Oxford: Oxford University Press.

Kessler, G., Rizzo, S., & Kelly, M. (2019, December 16). President Trump has made 15,413 false or misleading claims over 1,055 days. *The Washington Post*. Retrieved at: https://www.washingtonpost.com/politics/2019/12/16/president-trump-has-made-false-or-misleading-claims-over-days/.

Kiely, E., Robertson, L., Farley, R., & Gore, D. (2019, November 26). Flurry of Trump falsehoods. *Factcheck.org*. Accessed 12/9/19: https://www.factcheck.org/2019/10/flurry-of-trump-falsehoods/.

Leonhardt, D., & Thompson, S. A. (2017, December 14). Trump's lies. *New York Times*. Accessed 10/23/19: https://www.nytimes.com/interactive/2017/06/23/opinion/trumps-lies.html.

Levenson, E., Boyette, C., & Mack, J. (2020, March 12). Colleges and universities across the US are cancelling in person classes due to coronavirus. CNN. Accessed 3/12/20: https://www.cnn.com/2020/03/09/us/coronavirus-university-college-classes/index.html

Madrigal, A. C. (2018, May 30). When did TV watching peak? *The Atlantic*. Retrieved at: https://www.theatlantic.com/technology/archive/2018/05/when-did-tv-watching-peak/561464/.

McCombs, M. E. (2004). *Setting the agenda: The mass media and public opinion*. Cambridge: Polity.

McCombs, M. E., & Shaw, D. L. (1972). The agenda setting function of the mass media. *Public Opinion Quarterly*, *36*, 176–187.

Petrocik, J. R. (1996). Issue ownership in presidential elections, with a 1980 case study. *American Journal of Political Science*, *40*, 825–850.

Petrocik, J. R., Benoit, W. L., & Hansen, G. L. (2003–2004). Issue ownership and presidential campaigning, 1952–2000. *Political Science Quarterly*, *118*, 599–626.

Pittman, M., & Sheehan, K. (2015). Sprinting a media marathon: Uses and gratifications of binge watching television through Netflix. *First Monday*, *20*(10). Retrieved at: https://firstmonday.org/article/view/6138/4999.

Scheufele, D. A. (2000). Agenda-setting, priming, and framing revisited: Another look at cognitive effects of political communication. *Mass Communication & Society*, *3*, 297–316.

Wanta, A., & Ghanem, S. (2007). Effects of agenda-setting. In R. W. Preiss, B. M. Gayle, N. Burrel, M. Allen, & J. Bryant (Eds.), *Mass media effects research: Advances through meta-analysis*. Mahwah, NJ: Lawrence Erlbaum.

Index

Note: References to tables, figures, and boxes are indicated by an italic *t*, *f*, or *b* following the page number

Lee B. Becker, *General Editor*

The Mass Communication and Journalism series focuses on broad issues in mass communication, giving particular attention to those in which journalism is prominent. Volumes in the series examine the product of the full range of media organizations as well as individuals engaged in various types of communication activities.

Each commissioned book deals in depth with a selected topic, raises new issues about that topic, and provides a fuller understanding of it through the new evidence provided. The series contains both single-authored and edited works. For more information and submissions, please contact:

Lee B. Becker, Series Editor | *lbbecker@uga.edu*
Erika Hendrix, Commissioning Editor | *erika.hendrix@plang.com*

To order other books in this series, please contact our Customer Service Department:

peterlang@presswarehouse.com (within the U.S.)
order@peterlang.com (outside the U.S.)

Or browse online by series at www.peterlang.com